Reconcilable Differences
Marriages end. Families don't.

Reconcilable Differences

Marriages end.
Families don't.

Cate Cochran

with Janet Douglas Cochran

Second Story Press

Library and Archives Canada Cataloguing in Publication

Cochran, Cate, 1955-
Reconcilable differences : marriages end, families don't /
by Cate Cochran.

ISBN 978-1-897187-29-6

1. Divorced parents—Canada. 2. Children of divorced parents—
Canada. 3. Broken homes—Canada. 4. Family—Canada. I. Title.

HQ814.C62 2007   306.890971   C2007-903518-3

Cover design by Cate Cochran
Cover and Chapter 10 illustration © Joseph Sherman
Author photo © Edward Gajdel
Text design by Melissa Kaita

Printed on 100% post-consumer recycled paper
(Ancient Forest Friendly, FSC Certified)

Printed and bound in Canada

*Second Story Press gratefully acknowledges the support of the Ontario Arts
Council and the Canada Council for the Arts for our publishing program. We
acknowledge the financial support of the Government of Canada through the
Book Publishing Industry Development Program.*

ONTARIO ARTS COUNCIL
CONSEIL DES ARTS DE L'ONTARIO

Canada Council   Conseil des Arts
for the Arts   du Canada

Published by
SECOND STORY PRESS
20 Maud Street, Suite 401
Toronto, Ontario, Canada
M5V 2M5
www.secondstorypress.ca

To Joe, Maddie and Jake

And to my mother,
Janet Douglas Cochran

Contents

Introduction

WHEN I SPLIT UP WITH MY HUSBAND, one thing was certain: I did not want a crash-and-burn separation. Neither did he. We had friends whose marriages had disintegrated into rancor and vitriol; one couple's angry divorce dance became so animated it completely overshadowed their new lives. My husband and I vowed we would never allow that to happen to us. It seemed like a reasonable decision at the time. Later we realized how profoundly important that commitment would be.

When you stand on the threshold of a separation, it's like being at the edge of a forest fire. What you see and feel is intense heat, turmoil, and a force that appears beyond your control — a dangerous place, full of fear and loss. Emotions are in flux, there are major financial and legal issues to resolve and custody arrangements to be negotiated. There is so much to do, all in the midst of painful circumstances. But ending a marriage need not devastate a family. You don't have to destroy your children or your relationship with your former spouse. The family that remains doesn't have to be "broken."

⁀⁀

A forest fire seems to destroy everything in its path, but within three months, new life emerges from the charred forest floor. It takes time, but the forest re-establishes itself, and families can, too. I know this because I've been there. As I've learned, others have too. None of us wants to go through a divorce, but sadly, at least half of all marriages fail. The expectation is that it will be a hellish experience in which we and the person we once loved become adversaries and forget all that drew us to each other in the first place, but as the couples in this book show us, it doesn't have to be that way.

You'll see from their stories that it *is* possible to reconfigure a family so that it's functional and happy and loving. It will take time and patience, and sometimes the task will be extremely challenging. But once everyone regains their balance and emotions become calmer, you can transcend what did not work, preserve what did, and create something new that better meets everyone's needs. It will look and feel different, but that's okay.

Which is not to say it's an easy process to separate amicably. My husband and I hit many rough spots as we began to
reorganize the life that we'd shared for almost twenty years.
There were times, lots of them, when we could have blown
the family apart, but we didn't. Instead, we held close the
belief that we could rebuild a dysfunctional marriage into a
functioning family, and we did.

Sometimes support for our efforts was a little thin.
Some in the outside world told us we were being naive or
downright foolish. Books I read by "experts" predicted dire
consequences for our children, which was both demoralizing
and frightening. There were endless tales about how far wrong
people could go in ending their marriages, but there were no
mentors, no guides, and no reference texts for what we were
trying to do. We had to invent our own rules every step of the
way, and sometimes the odds against us seemed high.

In our separation, inspiration came from an unexpected
source: I loved playing house. As a toddler, I used to play with
saucepans and preserving jars, pretending the pans were
houses, the jars little grown-ups, and the lids the jar-people's
children. I'd take them to my bedroom at nap time, arrange
them in families, and create scenarios about who belonged
where, who lived with whom, and what all these people were
doing together. When I was a little older, I'd get into bed at
night, shake out my blanket, and watch as it settled into place
over my legs. How it landed determined the topography of
my stories. Its wrinkles were the walls of buildings that I'd
populate with tiny pretend people — mothers and fathers and

two or three children — because that's how I thought families looked. They'd talk and negotiate, grow up, get married, have babies, raise families, and sometimes even die. They lived on that woolen stage night after night, and each time I threw my blanket in the air a new world would fall in my lap.

As I grew up, my childhood game evolved into an ongoing curiosity about why and how people choose to live together. When I was thirty, I read a magazine article about American mystery writer Robert B. Parker and his wife, writer Joan H. Parker, who survived the breakdown of their marriage by buying a fourteen-room house with two apartments — one for him, one for her. Living in their own separate spaces, they were able to sidestep conflicts and renew their relationship. I loved the idea that they could *choose* when they wanted to be together, arranging to go on dates or inviting each other for dinner.

Then I heard about Canadian gardening writer Marjorie Harris and her husband, writer Jack Batten, who had restructured their lives after a difficult separation. When they reconciled, they dated for a while, then decided to share one house again after they wearied of shuttling between two homes and carrying two mortgages. They adopted an "upstairs-downstairs" arrangement, in which each had a separate apartment. The solution was unorthodox but workable, and they were happy. Both of these ideas seemed like good arrangements for a marriage, and I used to joke with my husband that we should move into side-by-side duplexes.

These stories informed an art project I undertook with another artist. We imagined what unconventional families might look like, and how they might live together. We researched unusual arrangements, created various scenarios, wrote narratives for each, and built dollhouse-sized replicas of each family's home. When the exhibit opened, gallery-goers could peek in the windows of six houses that on the outside looked identical but on the inside portrayed many different configurations of family life.

All these ideas became inspiration for my husband and me as we tried to design our new life as a separated couple raising children together. Hovering over cups of tea at our kitchen table, we talked about options, laughed that the side-by-side duplex might become a reality after all, and wondered if perhaps we could subdivide the house we were living in. We played with ideas, giving our bruised hearts some time to mend and allowing ourselves to imagine new possibilities. We told ourselves we didn't have to rush because we had to get it right. We promised to hold on to what mattered to *us* as parents and former partners, and this principle infused every decision we made about reconfiguring our nuclear family. And always — always — our bottom line was clear: our children would come first.

On some days, the whole undertaking was daunting at best, paralyzing at worst, but we refused to follow prescribed rules or surrender to fear, and there were times when I felt an almost giddy pride in ignoring the critics while designing a new life based on our own priorities.

In the beginning ours was a solitary journey, but as we talked with friends about what we were doing, we began to hear of other couples who had regrouped in unusual ways. Anecdotes told at dinner parties, asides shared over coffee — I devoured them all. Each story demonstrated that it was possible to rebuild a broken marriage into something that worked, even if it *was* off the grid. Those stories were an antidote to the poisonous tales we'd heard and I found them endlessly reassuring.

My husband and I did manage to restructure our family and now, four years later, we still live in an upstairs-downstairs arrangement that has worked very well for all of us — him, me, our two teenagers, and the dog. There have, of course, been bumps along the way and, even with a shared vision, some spectacular tumbles.

It's been said that you have to make stepping-stones out of stumbling blocks, and I believe that, but I also know what the bruises feel like after you've tripped. Even our best intentions could not prevent some tears and tantrums, and it took patience and kindness and much deep breathing as we regrouped. We did our best to conceal our frustrations from the children, and we all learned that angry words often masked fear, and ill will was the front man for insecurity. In time we began to understand that goodwill and a well-timed apology could overcome animosity. Gradually friendship replaced friction, and laughter and trust came back into our lives.

I wrote a magazine article about our experiences, a version of which appears as Chapter Ten of this book. In response to the magazine article some people commented that our story was anomalous and was only possible because we were unusual people. While I knew that our "experiment" broke with tradition, I never believed we were all that different from any other couple.

When I began to write this book, I looked for other similar families. I found some by chance, some through word of mouth, some who were referred to me, and some who sought me out after reading my article or hearing my story on the radio. As I began to interview these families about their own unorthodox experiments, I soon realized that there was no single model for restructuring a family. What they all had in common was that they had trusted themselves to know what was possible and sustainable. They'd all had the wit to take into account their own collective needs and the will to create a new working family that would function for them. They did it privately and without fanfare, and that clinched my belief that their stories deserved to be shared.

I chronicled each family's experiences in their own words, searching for successes rather than failures. I wanted to document the unique decisions that had been made by these divorce dissenters, who had insisted on exiting a marriage as graciously as possible. As I listened to their stories, I was astonished by what each family had accomplished. These were true relationship pioneers who had undertaken unique, often quirky solutions that worked for their families, and persevered in spite of their own insecurities and the chorus of doubters standing on the sidelines. Some had sustained their new family arrangements for more than ten years; others were just beginning their odyssey.

The topography of each family's journey through separation and divorce is pieced together through interviews with ex-spouses, children, and new partners. I asked grown children how they felt about being hauled along on their parents' experiments. I asked new partners what it was like to integrate into unusual arrangements. I quizzed former spouses about how they managed to rethink their relationship with an ex, and, where necessary, rein in their tempers and tame hurts and jealousies.

People shared intimate details of their lives and their struggles as they learned new rules: how to feel about each other, how to talk to each other, and how to treat each other with respect. Their stories are full of anger, pain, guilt, and fear — enough to hobble even the most diligent efforts to end a marriage well — but they're also crammed full of hope. After each interview, I'd shake my head in awe and amazement. I wondered why people were willing to disclose so much, but over time I began to understand that they were proud of what they had accomplished and wanted others to know what was possible.

Every one of us going through separation and divorce understands painful loss and a kind of manic terror. Tennessee Williams once described the process of writing a play as "frantically constructing another world while the world that you live in dissolves beneath your feet, and . . . your survival depends on completing this construction at least one second before the old habitation collapses." That's what the early days of rebuilding a family feels like.

And then there is the minefield of expert opinion. Every parent worries that we might be hurting our children by leaving our marriages — and no wonder. Early on in my separation, I thumbed through a book called *What About the Kids?* by Judith Wallerstein and Sandra Blakeslee and read, "With your divorce, true shared parenting evaporates. You have no one to call for help." They said, for instance, that when a child acts up in school, "you certainly can't say, 'I want to talk this problem over with my husband.'" I found this to be confounding advice. I asked myself why we as parents *wouldn't* continue to share responsibility and talk about our children — after all, we made those children together. Why should the end of our marriage signal the end of communication with each other?

Eventually I found a book called *The Good Divorce* by Constance Ahrons, in which the advice had a markedly different tone. She didn't sugarcoat the fact that divorce is tough, but she insisted that romance must catch up to the reality that "marriage and family are no longer synonymous," and "divorce is here to stay. It cannot be cured." Reading those words bolstered my belief that if so many of us are having to deal with this conundrum, there had to be a way to do the right thing for our children *and* ourselves. A friend once observed that couples often "live apart together while raising kids." If people can pull that off, wonderful, but some of us can't stay in marriages that wear out or become hazardous to our emotional health.

Ahrons herself had endured a destructive divorce, so it

really caught my attention when she said: "The good divorce is not an oxymoron. A good divorce is one in which both the adults and children emerge at least as emotionally well as they were before the divorce." This simple message bolsters my belief that marriages end, but families don't.

What I've learned through my own experiences and those of the families I've written about is that change has an ebb and a flow. Some days are easy, some are downright hard. Just as grief is an experience to be endured, we all have to learn to adapt to losing what we once felt would be permanent. To quote Ahrons again: "The stresses of losing roles, rules, and rituals in one fell swoop; the ambiguity that is perpetuated by the lack of adequate role models; the physical and financial stresses; the non-recognition by society — all these make constructing a bi-nuclear family an enormous, frequently overwhelming, but sometimes exhilarating, challenge."

Sometimes the exhilaration comes in unexpected ways. In my reconfigured family, there have often been moments of happiness embedded in the small details of a day. For instance, one evening our thirteen-year-old daughter Maddie was feeling unwell and crawled into bed with me for comfort. As we nestled together reading, her dad, who was worried about his little girl, tapped on the front door of my apartment. We invited him in, and he was able to check on how she was, feel her forehead, and have a brief conversation with her before he kissed her good night and headed back upstairs to his place. I knew in that moment of co-parenting our child just how worthwhile our arrangement is.

Ahrons also speaks of the importance of flexibility in successfully constructing a bi-nuclear family. In our case, each parent has a weekly set of responsibilities, but can pinch-hit for the other if something comes up. It was Joe, my ex-husband, who took over kid duty while I was writing this book so I could hide myself away somewhere and write. When I was getting the book ready to go to the publisher, I put on my art director's hat to do some layouts for the cover and Joe, who is an animator, was doing the illustration. One evening we were working side by side on the cover on two computers in his studio, me asking Joe for his input on colors and typefaces and Joe showing me his illustration as it progressed. Our daughter wandered into the studio, watched over our shoulders for a while, and then offered her feedback on the designs and the drawing. This book has been truly a family effort.

As you read these chapters, you'll see how the couples all reshaped their lives so there was room for everyone. These families are inspiring examples of people who live what they believe and who have had the courage, temerity, and faith to reinvent themselves.

— Cate Cochran

CHAPTER ONE

Through the Looking Glass

"I wanted to get one of those movable signs
and put it on the front lawn saying, 'Phil is okay.
We don't have him tied up in the basement,
and we're not feeding him gruel.'"

– Kathleen

KATHLEEN AND PHIL had no intention of becoming relationship pioneers when their marriage collapsed; they just wanted
out of a stale relationship. Up to then, their family had looked
like the "nuclear family" was supposed to look: two involved
parents, three happy kids, and a comfortable home in a nice
neighborhood. But when they called it quits, they made a bold
choice that put them on the very frontier of unusual family
arrangements.

Their life together had begun unremarkably. They were
university sweethearts who had moved in together after
graduation, set up housekeeping for a couple of years, and

married when they were ready to have children. Phil was a successful accountant and Kathleen a stay-at-home mom. They were "normal" with a capital "N."

Not that either of them had come from ordinary backgrounds. Kathleen had been raised in a household that questioned mainstream values, and she and her siblings were imbued with a sense of "freedom within boundaries." Kathleen remembers that the house was always full of "strays" — an uncle who came for extended visits, teenagers who camped in the basement. The core of the family was solid, but its boundaries were porous and flexible, often including an unusual cast of characters.

Phil, on the other hand, grew up in a traditional, rule-bound British family. Shortly after he was born his mother contracted tuberculosis, and for the first four years of his life he was raised by a nanny. His father was a driven, "stiff upper lip" kind of man, advisor to many but friend to few. In a family that was typical of the Fifties, his dad worked very hard, was away a lot, and was emotionally inaccessible, while his mother was always "impossibly angry" with his father, though never able to leave him. She maintained a gracious public persona but in private drank heavily, and both she and her husband died alcoholic and angry. Phil and his siblings learned early that strained silence was the easiest way to cope.

It was liberating for Phil to meet Kathleen. He had spent years at a boys' boarding school and was painfully unsure of himself, sexually and in relationships, and he was swept off his feet by the female energy of this attractive, fit woman full of offbeat ideas. To Phil, Kathleen was "a breath of fresh air — someone who spoke her mind and had opinions," and when she said she wanted to marry him, he remembers, "I was toast. That was it."

⟡

Kathleen and Phil moved enthusiastically into their roles as parents. Phil sewed the kids' Halloween costumes and made sure he was home for dinner every night, even if he had to go back to work after the children were in bed. Kathleen loved being a mother. She remembers waking up when the kids were young with a sense of well-being that she was following all the rules for the first time in her life and reaping lots of approval — baking muffins, taking part in the neighborhood garage sale, attending the kids' school council meetings, and thinking to herself, "I'm doing this quite well. Oh my God, how did this happen? I didn't expect to be living this perfect life."

But their "perfect life" was fragile, and both Kathleen and Phil sensed it long before they spoke of it to each other. The contrasting qualities that had drawn them together eventually began to divide them, and they started moving in different directions. They still had a joint life through the church, the school, and raising their kids, but there wasn't a lot of emotional interaction other than anger. Looking back, Phil thinks that they coexisted the way young children do: playing together but doing their own thing.

For Kathleen, the marriage was never awful, just neutral,

and they both began looking for fulfillment outside the marriage. They embraced Eighties-style "New Age" ideas, read stacks of self-improvement books, and talked about how to become perfect parents. They had beautiful kids and afflu- ence, but the sexual energy had become muted, and Kathleen knew "there was a wild woman in me that hadn't been around for a while."

She remembers it as a strange time. She and Phil had joined a couples' group and she had a flirtation with one of the men. It helped her get in touch with her sexual energy, but she realized that she didn't want to have an affair. At the same time, she was doing her own group therapy and discovered that one of the women in the group had a crush on her. She remembers that "all this talk kind of swirled around, and the feelings were there, and it's almost like I was figuring this stuff out on a back burner, because on the front burner I was working it out with Phil."

Phil was also feeling the strain of their dissolving marriage, but radical change was not on his agenda. "I don't think I had the strength to leave," he says. "I don't think I could have withstood the anger or disappointment from the kids, and I certainly wasn't strong enough to face Kathleen's fury."

Thirteen years down the road the marriage imploded when Kathleen went to look at a cottage that she and Phil were think- ing of buying. She took along her best friend, Jane, and over the weekend the two women found themselves involved with each other in a way that would change everyone's lives forever. Jane had been secretly in love with Kathleen for eighteen years, and for her it was the realization of a dream. For Kathleen it was the discovery of a whole new part of herself and it gave her back something that she'd lost in her marriage. "I know this isn't a story about how I came out as a lesbian, but it was finding my sexual energy that led me to the break with Phil."

Having his wife fall in love with another woman might have devastated Phil, but it didn't. He had also been unfulfilled within the marriage, and when Jane and Kathleen confided their news he was quick to recognize his own escape route. Pragmatism and the desire to be with his children overrode any anger he might have felt about being rejected by his wife. Their relationship had not been in great shape for quite some time and Phil viewed the news as an opportunity to split up, gain brownie points, and still keep his kids.

Phil's nature tends to be reactive rather than proactive. Instead of moving out he volunteered to sleep in the basement, where there was a bedroom and bathroom. He recalls that it was actually a relief to go downstairs — like having a room of one's own. "I'll deal with a situation and deal with it and deal with it, and then at some point it becomes unbearable and an opening happens and just like water I'll go for the opening. I didn't really think a whole lot about my ego. You know how water runs downhill? I wanted an emotional downhill. In the perception of everybody else, I was kicked out downstairs and I did the honorable thing: I stayed around."

For Kathleen, this was a chance to exit her marriage without destroying her family. Phil was remarkably loving and supportive, and she credits him with seeing that if they hadn't altered course they'd have become disappointed old people. He knew that neither of them was satisfied and while he didn't want the family to break up, he understood why they needed to make a change. From Jane's perspective, "It was all very unorthodox — a case of 'getting out' and 'coming out' that worked for everyone."

This unconventional arrangement was a civilized approach, and in the adult world, it made sense. But to three little children whose lives were being turned inside out, it didn't. They were not happy. The world as they knew it changed forever, and it happened very quickly. Almost in the same breath, the children learned that their parents were splitting up and that their mother had a new partner — a woman.

⁂

Three months later, Jane moved in. She and Kathleen slept on the second floor where the kids' bedrooms were located, while Phil stayed in the basement. The children's reactions varied. Jessie, who was nine, and Christopher, who was eleven, were livid. Maggie, who was just six, adapted most easily, feeling little insecurity because for her very little had changed. She remembers feeling sad that her dad was in the basement, but was comforted that he was still in the house. And she loved his basement room — it felt so safe. In the morning, she'd wake up and hear him calling upstairs: "What do you want for lunch?" For her that was fun, sort of like a game. Her dad was there every morning when she came down for breakfast, and was home for dinner at night, so life had a familiar shape.

The adults in the new configuration quickly agreed on ground rules that according to Kathleen had an elegant and compelling simplicity. "The founding premise for all of the changes that came next was Phil and I saying that we were not going to live without our children. We both knew how important they were to us and how important we were to them, and we knew that we had to find another way of making the family work."

So the household shifted into a different gear and functioned remarkably well. Jane recalls the arrangement with fondness: "We ate all our meals together and we shared the grocery shopping. It was like living in a co-op. And Phil was a part of everything. We lived as a family, vacationed as a family, shared the load, and had compatible living habits — all those things that make a household work."

People sometimes wondered how Jane could live with this arrangement, but Jane had no illusions about her status. She understood the deal. She had wanted to live with Kathleen, and this was the price of entry. "Okay, fine," she quipped. "I've got to live with your spoiled children and your ex-husband, too. If you ever wondered whether I was devoted or not, this is devoted, right?"

The kids had always been given a very powerful voice in what happened because they were at the center of Kathleen and Phil's universe, Jane explains, and the relationship with the kids was way more important than their own relationship. "That was the dynamic that I came into," she says, "so for our relationship, Kath's and mine, to be sidelined was not unusual. They were used to the grown-up relationships not really mattering."

Jane believes she was able to accept her second-class status partly because she'd grown up lesbian and marginalized. "I think that was critical to my being able to live in the shadows the way I did. As long as I felt secure in the romantic connection I could live with that other stuff. He's their father, you're their mother, and I'm this other thing." She worked hard to get the children to like her and is now very close to the kids.

The home was rambunctious, loud, and expressive. The struggles were noisy, and when the children weren't happy the whole house knew it. Regular family meetings often degenerated into no-holds-barred battlegrounds. Phil hated getting dragged into these conversations. The battles weren't Jane's way of dealing with things, either. "I am not a yeller. In personality and temperament, Phil and I are much more similar," Jane acknowledges. When things got rough and conversations became difficult, she'd find tasks while the maelstrom went on around her — she folded a lot of laundry and cooked many meals.

The meetings were set up so that everyone had a chance to air their views, and Kathleen insisted they were an important opportunity to sort things out. "I think that if you ask the adults," she says, "you'll find that I'm the bitch of the piece. I'm the one who has the temper. I'm the one who is volatile. I'm the one who cried the most and was most difficult to deal with. But I believe I'm also the one who held it together at different junctures because I wasn't willing to let it go."

For Kathleen, building this new entity was a crusade; for Phil, it was a question of taking the path of least resistance in order to be with his children; and for Jane, the newcomer to the family, it was a matter of "take it or leave it."

❧

There were times when figuring out this new set of relationships was fraught with confusion, anger, and fear, but it was also a process that was infused with goodwill and good faith. There were some tensions around money, though, because Kathleen made none and Phil made a whole lot. Phil could see that Kathleen was terrified that she was going to wake up under a bridge, and he tried to defuse the fear. They eventually worked out their financial issues amicably and when they settled, Kathleen got half the assets and Phil took all the debts. "It was never a problem, just not an issue," he says.

Their concord was solid, but sometimes external pressures rattled them. Kathleen was fearful that Phil's strong-willed father would get a court order to remove the kids from her custody because she was a lesbian. But Phil had no doubt where he stood with the kids, so he gave her sole custody. He saw them every day, knew they wanted to see him, and was confident that Kathleen wanted him to see them.

Nor did he and Kathleen rush to bring lawyers onto the scene. They took some pleasure in controlling the legal process when it came to formalizing their arrangement. Phil still smiles with satisfaction at the memory. "Our lawyers were so pissed off at us because they didn't know how to deal with us. We drafted a one-and-a-half page separation agreement which, when I look at it now, is just laughable. I can use the term 'New Age' because it's just got granola written all over it: 'We love each other, but we don't love each other enough to stay married, and we love the kids, and we love life and everything's good.'" Putting this formal agreement into place was a matter of getting in and out of the lawyers' offices as quickly as possible. The meeting was over in forty-five minutes.

ॐ

The outside world seemed to have more trouble dealing with their situation than they did. People seemed perplexed — even threatened — with their new family arrangement, and Jane still bristles at the way they reacted. "The sympathy went to Phil, especially when he was living in the basement. There were people, including his mother, who thought we had some kinky, three-way thing going on. There were people in the neighborhood who disapproved, so they said they were worried about the children. But I think a lot of their judgment went way beyond the needs of the children, who continued to excel at school and sports and everything else they'd always done. I was probably the first lesbian most of them had met and, in this configuration, I was certainly the home-wrecker, so I had the experience of people really avoiding me on the street."

Kathleen often fantasized about getting a sign for the front lawn that said "Phil is okay. We don't have him tied up in the basement, and we're not feeding him gruel. He's having a pretty good time. He's got a fairly good deal here. There's somebody raising his kids who has got a brain and is looking after the creature comforts and creating a home, for whatever that's worth."

She suspected there were some insidious factors at work here. "I honestly believe that people would have understood better if Phil and I had been in a fight and one of us had been the wronged party. But we both said the other was great, that we still cared for each other, and that the kids were the most important thing. I think that made people very uncomfortable. That's why it's important that these stories get told, because there are other stories like ours, and people keep them secret because there's a shame around doing things a different way."

Jessie and Maggie attended a group for children of divorce and it quickly became clear that they were not experiencing divorce the way other children were. Kathleen remembers her kids coming home looking shell-shocked, saying, "Mommy, you wouldn't believe what some kids have had to put up with and how they're treated. We feel so lucky." Kathleen never consciously portrayed their new family as perfect, but emphasized that they were really trying to work things out. She acknowledges, though, that they did make some mistakes.

Looking back, everyone agrees the transition from one family grouping to another was too rushed. In the early stages, the kids found it tough to manage the structure, and it might have made sense to allow them more time to adjust to the new circumstances. This household had always teemed with its own passionate energies, and one night, while Phil was dealing with the hubbub of cranky kids, things became so chaotic that Kathleen and Jane crawled into the closet in their bedroom and hid amongst their shoes to wait out the storm.

Chris had inherited his mother's volatile nature and was constantly in head-on collisions with all of the adults in the house, particularly his mother. He felt he'd been dragged into his parents' experiment and expressed his anger and frustration with great drama. He saw Jane as the interloper and remembers testing Jane as a rite of passage. "If this person was going to be part of the family, she needed to not get freaked out by my ability to get very angry. I don't think many people would have put up with what she put up with. Whatever you can think of — names, swear words or negative words about lesbians — I was calling my mother and Jane these things." Under his anger, though, there was a scared little boy. On a ski trip, he plaintively asked if he could have his old family back. He wanted the experiment to be over and to return to the way things were. It fell to Kathleen to disabuse him of that idea.

ల్>

Unbeknownst to his family, there was another dynamic at work for Chris. He had begun questioning his own sexuality. Jane vividly remembers that challenging period. "We had a very rough five years. Christopher identified closely with his family, his mother in particular, and seemed to feel that 'if *she* is, then they're going to know *I* am, and my cover's been blown.'"

Jane understood viscerally his torment and his need to deny that he was gay. "Like all of us who knew very young, he worked very hard not to be. Why would you want to be gay if you didn't have to?" Like many young people, Chris came out when he went to university, and Jane finds it interesting that growing up in a gay family didn't fast track him at all in terms of coming to terms with his sexuality.

Chris remembers that carrying his secret alone isolated him from the people most important to him. "To expose how our family was different also made me think about how I was different from my friends." When he came out and started to tell his family what he had gone through, it was painful for Kathleen "because I had burdened him with this other thing." Still, she believes it was actually harder for the children to deal with the fact that their parents were separating than that she was a lesbian.

Chris's relationship with his father had always been strained. Phil's behavior seemed quirky, which didn't help a boy who longed for a "regular" sporty dad. "He was riding his bike to work with a milk crate on it and living in the basement — things I didn't associate with being a strong man," Chris says. "It's interesting that that kind of sexism fed into the negative view I had of my dad. Our connection was rocky, but if he had moved out we would have had even less of a base to work on when I started to grow up."

Maggie was by nature an observer, quiet and introverted. "I needed a lot of time by myself, and I just didn't know what to do with all the noise. I didn't know how to get my voice into all of that." She used to sing at family meetings, because she was too little to contribute words. As the youngest in the house she watched from the shadows, seeing how tough it was for the adults in her life to break new ground, but she admired them for trying. "As I get older, I'm realizing how difficult it is to go against the grain without feeling completely vulnerable. I've definitely had my moments of wishing that things had been more straightforward but I don't know any different so it's hard to get pissed off about your life, about the whole situation, because it just *is*. There's nothing I could have done about it."

Jessie often took out her frustrations on Jane. "My relationship with my mom has always been quite harmonious. We never fought a lot other than the regular . . . like my wanting to go to parties that I wasn't allowed to go to. I think I took most of my anger out on Jane, and she's always been able to push my buttons." The reverse was true too, and one memorable early morning conflict sent the imperturbable Jane slamming out of the house in a fury when Jessie told Jane she wasn't her stepmother and refused to get out of bed.

There were also times when the children just didn't know how to explain who was what to whom in this unusual arrangement. Maggie remembers a time when her friend Jen came over. When Jen asked who Jane was, Maggie told her she was the cleaning lady. She feels badly about that now but at the time she couldn't just say "she's my mom's partner, she's a lesbian."

⚜

Looking back now, both Jessie and Maggie agree that Jane was a parent from the moment she walked in the door. She was there all the time, cooked meals, helped with homework, did the laundry, and was just part of the daily routine. The children eventually settled down, Jane was accepted, and the new household began to chug along. It continued to be a busy place. The children were involved in numerous activities, and the adults settled into a routine of getting kids to and from lessons, dividing up the driving duties, and sharing parental responsibilities.

That continued for two years until Phil decided to move out of the basement and into a little house the family had bought kitty-corner to the main house. It was one of several alterations to the setup of the family that would take place over the years and, as usual, it was precipitated by a dramatic moment. Phil remembers it vividly. "Kathleen and I had an enormous fight and she said, 'Why don't you just move out of here and go to the other house,' and the door was open. I was gone two and a half weeks later."

Jane remembers it a little differently. "He wanted to live more like a grown-up, with more space, more quiet. This place was a madhouse and Phil likes a quieter life. He didn't go very far, but it made a difference. It meant the kids had to actually *go* there."

Still, Phil's move to the "little house" was nominal and the "big house" remained the hub of family activity. He slept at his place but had almost no furniture and was still at the big house a lot of the time.

The news that Phil would be moving out upset all of the children, especially Maggie, who was still a small child. "I freaked out," she says. "I wanted him close." Jessie remembers that he took them to a coffee shop to reveal his plans. "I don't remember why I got so upset. I guess that was the point that it became real to me that he wasn't with my mom anymore. Maybe before that I could pretend that it was all the same. I stormed out. I was really sad and scared because I was worried about him being lonely and in his own house and stuff. He was fine, obviously."

In the end, Maggie and Jessie did adjust because not a lot had changed. They were still living pretty much as a connected family. Kathleen fondly remembers waking in the morning to the sound of the key turning in the lock, when Phil would arrive before she was up and would get breakfast started and help get the kids dressed, much as he did when he lived there. "Gradually, as the kids got older and were getting themselves ready it didn't make sense for him to come over and make breakfast, but he would often stop by on his way home from work to have supper with us. That's never stopped."

For five years they continued to function as a family, even with Phil living apart. There were moments when Jane allowed herself to dream that things might be a little different. "I was proud that we were doing it this way, and it made for an interesting dynamic. But there were definitely times when I just wished that he wasn't at every meal."

❧

Many times over the years the children have taken issue with Kathleen for indulging in a kind of myth-making. She tries to understand their experience of all this while also factoring in the need to show them how badly things *could* have gone. "Maggie says that I wanted it to be perfect, and we have this family myth that it *was* perfect, and I know it wasn't. But I had to tell myself we were doing pretty well because I saw the horror stories around us."

Maggie struggled with her mother's need to look for the positive. To her, that relentlessly upbeat attitude restricted the range of reactions she could express about what they'd been through. "You can have your confrontations, you can fight, but you can't say 'I'm really sad that you and Dad got divorced.' There's so much guilt that the adults have . . . [and we have] to live that myth, so the adults can feel it's okay. And everything *is* fine, but that doesn't mean things aren't sad and hard."

One of the major landmarks in the life of the family was a flood. They had all gone away for the weekend and returned to find the big house under several feet of water. For the three months it took to renovate, the kids moved in with Phil, and Kathleen and Jane camped wherever they could find a dry spot in the big house. New routines began emerging as old ones were revised. All of the cooking took place in the little house because Jane and Kathleen didn't have a kitchen, although Kathleen still did the shopping and cooking. Phil took on the bedtime routines for the children, and that pushed the family to a new stage. After the big house was repaired, they set up a new schedule and the kids continued to eat at the little house and sleep there a couple of nights a week. The family continued to celebrate holidays together and even ventured en masse on a European vacation.

&

And then Phil met another woman. He and Sue had known each other professionally for many years, and five years to the day after Jane moved in with Kathleen, Phil and Sue went out together. "We had our first date April 1st, which I've always thought was highly appropriate," says Sue. "And if I'd had any idea, I would have thought it was even more appropriate. We had a lovely time. And then we had another date, and we just knew."

Kathleen and Sue couldn't be more different. Kathleen's five foot four, Sue's five foot nine, Kathleen's an athlete, and Sue is not, but the biggest difference is that Sue never raises her voice. Kathleen's more volatile, more outspoken and much more definite than Sue, although Sue admires these traits. Where Jane and Kathleen will do lots of processing to work things through, Sue is more interested in the result, and when Phil says he thinks they should talk about a problem, her attitude is, "Let's fix it and move on."

Within weeks Phil and Sue were an item, and it wasn't long before she was invited to meet the family. The occasion was a full-blown Easter dinner with everything that goes with it, and Sue thought it was amazingly good-natured of them. She was pleased to be included, but quickly recognized that there was more to the encounter than a good meal. Within two weeks of when they started dating, Sue already knew that Phil was part of this family unit and that she would be part of that unit too. Phil had been really clear about that: "This is how it works, because this is my way to stay connected to my kids. This is incredibly important to me, my kids are more important to me than anything else."

That dinner was a pleasant start to a rocky voyage. Kathleen felt threatened by the arrival of another woman on the scene. She wasn't sure how this would shift the balance they'd worked hard to establish, and her concern showed itself over seemingly trivial things. Jane remembers a quintessential moment that underscored Kathleen's insecurities about what role Sue would try to play with her children. "We were on the train to Montréal and we'd brought our lunch. Sue had worked in daycare for years, so when food appears, you try to make sure everyone's got a sandwich. Sue's clucking over the lunch, and Kath is steaming. That is so much *her* job. *She'd* made the lunch. And I'm sitting there thinking, 'Whoa, Sue, you are really overstepping the bounds.'"

Sue remembers this experience as particularly painful. "The sandwiches were under my chair, and at one point I said to the kids, 'Do you guys want a sandwich?' because it was obvious people were getting hungry. Well, you would have thought I had said, 'Would you like me to be your real mother?' There was an immediate scene and there was all this arguing, and I realized — big mistake."

Jane explains the dynamic this way. "Sue was now in the

privileged position as the partner of this wealthy heterosexual man in a much more socially acceptable family unit. She had what Kathleen had given up, really, and the only thing Kath had left of that was the kids. And if Sue and Phil really had wanted, they probably could have gotten the kids, too. That was the fear."

ᴄᴛᴏ

There were other challenges. The lack of borders, which was the hallmark of this family, made Sue uncomfortable. Boundary issues in relationships where two full-time parents are trying to stay attached to their children will always be extraordinarily difficult for the incoming partners, and a particularly farcical scene led to a major rethinking of those boundaries. "I was sleeping over at Phil's and was having a shower when I realized that Phil and Kath were having an argument about something. I thought it sounded really close, and I realized they were in the hallway on the second floor and all I knew was my clothes were in the master bedroom, I was in the bathroom, and there was a space between that was filled with two people. I didn't have any way of getting to the other end of the hall, and I really needed my clothes and I really needed to go to work.

"So I stuck my head out the door and said, 'Excuse me, can you guys take this downstairs?' They went downstairs, and I got dressed and left for work. When I came home I said to Phil, 'You can't do that. Your relationship with Kathleen is your business, but if I'm going to live in this house you can't fight in this house. I can't have that kind of relationship.' In retrospect it's sort of funny, but at the time it was just like, oh my God, what have I gotten myself into?"

Jane mourns the changes that resulted from that incident. Until then there had been lots of overlap between households but that changed, because it had to if Sue were going to stick around. Kathleen and Jane no longer had ready access to Phil's house. Sue wanted them to knock at the door. Phil started knocking at the big house, too, and Jane and Kathleen found it weird to have him knocking or phoning to ask if he could come over. They felt he was modeling what he wanted them to do. They withdrew into a congenial but slightly more distant and formal relationship.

One non-negotiable was communicated to Sue very quickly. No more children. "This never ever would have worked if either of the new partners had had children," Sue said. "Too complicated. Where would the other children have had a place? It just wouldn't have worked. For me, that was a real sacrifice."

Despite all of the bumps in the road, the unit of seven survived for a decade and a half. Over the years they had to recalibrate and find a new equilibrium to match evolving circumstances. Sue and Phil married, and Kathleen and Jane married. Sue's philosophical about it all. "You do the best you can do with the resources that you have available to you at the time . . . your emotional resources. Even when you're doing this difficult grown-up stuff in the best way you can for little kids, they're still going to be pissed. And it's still going to be confusing, and they're still going to wish that their mom and dad are together."

Maggie ponders the world she grew up in, the only one she remembers, and believes that it offered her some distinct if sometimes uncomfortable advantages. "I don't have any conventional kind of model. It's cool on the one hand because I'm not being shoved into this box, but it's terrifying because it leaves you not knowing and having to figure it out for yourself, which is important but really hard. My family model is not the norm, so I'm starting from the outside anyway. I've never felt comfortable in that conventional setting. I've tried it on, but it just doesn't work. I think that I've gained things from my two stepparents that other people who don't have divorced families wouldn't gain. I have four pretty cool adults in my life. I wouldn't have wanted my parents to stay in an unhappy relationship. I think that would have been damaging in its own way for us."

Chris, who had made Jane's life such hell, and who was old enough to remember life before his parents split up, developed a deep trust with Jane that led him to confide in her about some key parts of his life. Jane remembers that when Chris came home to tell his family he was gay, he said to her, "The only person I really wanted to tell was you, Jane, because I knew that would be easy, and telling them was going to be hard." Her calm nature and her place as a trusted adult also allowed him to confide in her about wanting to switch out of engineering and change universities. "It's almost as though my reserve, my standing back, means that I'm the person they come to when they want the non-spaz," Jane says. "They want to hear what Mom would think, but without the spaz factor thrown on it."

Since Kathleen's active community work eventually led her to politics, where she had a demanding and hectic schedule, Jane was the frontline person who was around when the children called or came home. "I have a really, really close relationship with the kids. And in the last few years, since Kathleen's political career really took off, Maggie and I have become very close. I have been the primary parent for her for the last four years, because I'm the one who's here."

Maggie, from the vantage point of her twenty-one years now, observes that the adults were doing their best. "It was always very clear that no matter what, they were always going to be there for us. There was definitely a lot of support. Just because a kid comes from a divorced family, that doesn't mean that the family's not supportive and not paying attention.

"It's a bizarre idea to think that staying in an unhappy situation is good, because kids know what's going on. It might not be said out loud, but we know. It's a bad scene all around. I think [you need to be] honest with yourself, no matter how hard it is, and that sounds so cheesy but it's true. If you can figure out a way to be happy, the pieces will fall into place. That's something that my family has definitely taught me — that you don't have to stay in a bad, unhappy situation. It doesn't have to be like that."

Jessie has a similar view with regard to her parents. "The perspective that I always had was that they were holding on to the relationship because it's what would be best for us. In the end, as the years have passed — and this is the part that makes me happy — you can see that they really do have fun together, and they held onto something there." Jane makes a similar observation. "There's a deep, deep affection there. They say they'll always be in each other's lives. They just will be."

Sue, who had to find her own place within this rowdy crew, also appreciates the impact of Phil's and Kathleen's more than civil relationship. "I think it would be fair to say that Phil and Kathleen made way better parents than they made partners. And their gift to the world is those three fabulous young adults. Now I think that they're pretty good friends, but that took awhile. There was a period of time when that was easier said than done, and now I think that it's easier said *and* done, which is a credit to both of them, and to their partners who have worked to make that happen as well."

❧

Over the years, the seven individuals in this dynamic family have had to adapt to many changes. But recently, things altered when Phil and Sue moved away from the neighborhood. It had always been in the plans that they would leave when the children had been fledged, but it was still a jolt for Kathleen. "They sold their house a year ago and moved downtown," she said. "Maggie was twenty. She was six when we started. It was sad. The family was changing, and there was a sense of loss in that."

But there's also a sweetness in the way things are now,

which Kathleen experienced when having dinner with Phil and Sue and Maggie not long ago. The mood was convivial and she describes how that felt. "It's a different sense of well-being, not the sense that comes from external approval but the sense that boy, I have these six other people in the world who really care, and that's a gift. It doesn't come easily to have that kind of connection."

And Phil? He has a graphic way of summing up what he values most. "Part of why I have a strong relationship with Jane and Kathleen and my kids is that they're family. When all else fails, when you get dry leprosy and your limbs start to fall off, family's there."

CHAPTER TWO

And the Kids Get the House

"In the past, people stayed together
for the kids. But you can have kids and still have
families without being miserable in your
marriage. There are other ways to do things."
— Julia

WHO KNOWS WHAT BROUGHT Esther Benaim's marriage
to an end — a midlife crisis? early menopause? relationship
fatigue? — but something short-circuited. She was married to
a man who loved her, a man she'd known since she was seventeen. They'd been together for more than two decades, and
had two beautiful children. But when she turned forty, it was
as if she'd crossed a line and her unhappiness began to leak
out all over the place. Dissatisfied and restless, overwhelmed
by her life as a mother and wife, something happened all of a
sudden. "I couldn't even eat," Esther remembers. "I started
to lose weight. I just started to feel different about myself,
wanting to change."

One day she found she was staring at an old woman cross-
ing the street, trying to imagine herself at that age. What
would she be like? Was she living the life she wanted to live?
Esther had known some unhappy times during the course of
her marriage and had experienced periods when the world
seemed bleak, but this was different. She couldn't shake the
dark feeling. "I figured it was just me because really, there
was nothing wrong. We didn't fight, we had similar interests,
he was very smart, and he loved me to death. So what was my
problem?"

Her problem was that she had maxed out. Her relationship with her husband wasn't sustaining her anymore,
and her day-to-day routine made her feel like she was on
an accelerating treadmill. She'd go to work, rush home to
prepare dinner, then rush back downtown to pick up kids
from ballet, "driving to this, driving to that, carpooling in the
middle of snowstorms." She remembers losing it one night
on the phone with another parent, saying, "I can't do this shit
anymore, I just can't." It was too much and she felt burned
out. "It was a wrenching period. The amount of crying that I
did was just unbelievable."

For some months Esther set about remaking herself and
struggled to decipher what wasn't working in her marriage.
She had lost the intimacy she had once known with her
husband, Duff, and she moved out of their bed and into her
own bedroom on the third floor.

She and Duff concocted stories to explain why they were
sleeping in separate rooms, none of which washed with their

daughter, eleven-year-old Julia, who knew when she was being conned. "I asked what was going on, and they gave me some bogus story about Dad snoring or Dad kicking. Okay, so they just realized that after twenty-three years? I was never a pull-the-wool-over-my-eyes type of kid, and right then and there I knew something was up."

This arrangement continued for about a year, until Duff couldn't stand it anymore and insisted they deal with the situation. It was a pivotal moment in their marriage, and Esther's response wasn't what Duff was expecting or hoping for. When put up against the wall, she just said, "That's it, I can't live like this any more."

She and Duff took a stab at redeeming their relationship and went into counseling, but they couldn't seem to fix things between them. Esther had begun to move in another direction and there was no going back. As much as Duff wanted to try to make it work, for Esther it was very similar to leaving her parents' house once her mother found her birth control pills. She couldn't live there anymore after that.

❧

Duff and Esther met through Duff's younger sister and over the years had become the kind of couple people speak of in one breath: Esther and Duff, Duff and Esther. They moved in together, and then one morning he said, "You know, I think we should be married." Esther laughs as she remembers her response. "I said, 'Yeah, sure. Why not?'" It was the early Seventies, and they were living the alternative lifestyle. "If you look at pictures of my mom and dad when they were younger, they were the biggest hippies," Julia says, describing snapshots from the family photo album. "My dad had this huge afro and my mom had the long straight hair parted in the middle, and they'd go camping and they'd backpack all over, smoke weed, do all this hippie stuff. My dad was in a band. He wanted to be a jazz musician."

As with many of their "radical" contemporaries, they broke some social rules and honored others. They did get married, but Esther insisted there be no traditional wedding — no place cards, no fussy wedding dress — and only one shower, where her friends gave her tools as presents. They were anti-everything at that time, but Esther knew how important it was to celebrate at least, so she bowed to pressure and wore a simple wedding gown made by her aunt, and even conceded to some beadwork on the dress. Esther is Moroccan, so they had Moroccan food and belly dancing, and people danced like crazy. Twenty years later, people still were talking about their wedding.

Instead of starting a family right away, Esther and Duff pursued other interests. They did everything together — cooking, traveling extensively, playing sports, and entertaining friends. Duff continued his schooling and became an engineer. Esther dabbled in various pastimes: setting up a quilt business; working in her sister-in-law's bakery; running cooking classes. And she wasn't going to have babies until she was good and ready. "It was my anti-establishment thing," she says, laughing at her own stubbornness. "Just because we were married didn't mean we had to have kids. I remember having a big argument with a cousin, who said, 'That's what you're supposed to do.' And I told her I never do what I'm supposed to do."

Ten years into their marriage, following a long trek overseas, Esther overcame her ambivalence about becoming a mother. She decided it was time to have kids, and she became pregnant right away. Julia was the first of two children, with Ben coming along five years later. Esther and Duff dove into parenting, sharing the duties however they could. For a while Esther was a full-time mother, and Duff a fully involved father who was always there. Even in the five years that Esther was at home, Duff would come home after work and pitch right in, cleaning up if she had made dinner, and taking Julia out on bike rides. Those outings on the bicycle figure largely in Julia's memory of her father. "If you look back in family albums you'll see a lot of pictures of me and my dad when I was a baby. I used to have a basket on the back of his bike and he'd ride around everywhere with me in the basket. I guess I was daddy's girl."

Duff and Esther shared a natural affinity for parenting, but along the way their own relationship began to coast. By the time they noticed, it had drifted beyond reach. Their final parting was heartrending, and not Duff's choice, but however difficult it was for them to sever their emotional ties, they managed to avoid open clashes. They knew that they didn't want to go to war. That wasn't the way that they dealt with each other, ever. They were civil. Some couples find it possible to remain friendly after a split, but it was challenging for Duff and Esther. "It was just too painful, but we knew that we were going to try, no matter what, because the kids were first."

It was difficult for Esther to maintain equilibrium when she was so aware that she'd made a decision that might protect *her* sanity, but that would have a huge impact on her family. She had never anticipated finding herself in a situation where she would leave her husband, but suddenly "everything was intense, because I was breaking up my life. The guilt over the kids was just tremendous. I still feel it."

Esther and Duff's standoff remained a private one and from Julia's standpoint, relations between the adults in the house were peaceful. In stark contrast, Julia had witnessed bitter battles taking place between another couple who were close to the family. "I remember sleeping over at their house and the parents screaming at each other in the middle of the night and I heard all their private business — just crazy arguments. I called my parents and told them to come and get me. I remember not feeling safe in that house. I lost all respect for that man that night, but I never lost respect for my dad or my mom because I never heard either of them speak to each other that way. There was never any big fighting between them and I never heard one argument, so I think that they are both extremely good people."

e⁓ɔ

Esther and Duff began the laborious process of deciding how to separate, and what to do about making arrangements for the children. Their challenge would be to create a situation that would facilitate an uneasy peace. Sadly, theirs wasn't going to be the kind of separation that would result in a convivial relationship. "It was totally uncomfortable," Esther confessed. "He didn't want the break-up, so he was angry, he was sad. It was better that we didn't cross paths." Neither indulged in mudslinging, though. They cooperated when and how they could, and maintained enough distance to allow themselves to grieve the loss of a relationship that had once been so solid and happy.

They discussed a shared custody arrangement, but the idea of shuttling the children back and forth between them didn't feel right, nor did giving greater access to one parent or the other. Duff wasn't about to be a weekend parent. Esther didn't want to be and didn't expect Duff to be, because he was much too involved as a father to ever do that. One day, during a meeting in her lawyer's office, Esther had a brainwave. Why not reverse the standard arrangement of moving the kids, and have the parents do the coming and going instead? What Esther had stumbled upon was the idea for a "bird's nest" arrangement, which was very unusual in the 1980s. Instead of moving the children between houses, the family home would be the fulcrum. This was an appealing option because it minimized the disruption her children would experience — no bags to pack, no shifting gears between homes — and it offered Esther, who had grown up as one of five siblings in a crowded two-bedroom apartment, an alluring kind of independence she had never experienced. Duff agreed to the idea and they began to hammer out some details. Not knowing anyone else who had tried this kind of setup, they were complete tenderfoots. They considered keeping the house and getting one apartment they could share, but Esther needed a space of her own, where she wouldn't constantly be reminded of Duff and their life together. Eventually they agreed that they would each get an apartment and keep their own bedrooms in the family home. It was an expensive option, but they thought they could make it work and agreed to try it.

❧

Then they had to tell the children. Julia was twelve, Ben only seven. Both children cried, and Julia was angry with her parents. "It wasn't a total shock. I was anticipating it, but when it actually came I was still pretty upset. I was crying a lot, I was angry, I don't know at who. I wasn't mad at them for their marriage not working, but I was mad that they had tried to hide it." The lack of transparency during that time isn't something Esther feels good about. She had been going to a therapist, but being non-confrontational by nature, she wasn't able to speak openly about what was going on.

Julia didn't want to be home after hearing the news. For the next few days she stayed with a friend whose parents had been divorced a long time. Divorce was so prevalent in Julia's peer group that when she looks back she hardly remembers any kids who lived in an intact nuclear family. "I've seen so much of it. I think I might have one or two friends whose parents are still married . . . out of all those I've ever been friends with . . . out of everybody I've met."

Family life for Julia had been in a kind of suspended animation for almost a year while her parents were trying to sort themselves out. She had adapted to the "new normal," but she mourned the news of their actual separation because it meant an end to the life she'd known. She was afraid of what her parents' divorce would mean to the family, and she fretted about hypothetical scenarios. She worried about how she would explain things to her own children, if she ever had any. She also worried about the details of day-to-day living. "I kept saying, 'What am I going to do, live out of a suitcase? I don't want to live out of a suitcase,' because I had so many friends who were doing that. I kept saying, 'This is going to ruin my life. What if I forget something at my mom's house and then I have to go to my dad's?' I guess I was pretty selfish. I was only thinking about me and what effect it would have on my life." Esther and Duff reassured the kids that they would not be living the life of vagabonds.

Once they had their plan in place, Esther and Duff began the process of making it a reality. The idea of having a private space of her own may have been lovely in Esther's imagination, but once she hit the pavement looking for a new nest for herself, finding something she could afford was less dreamy. "It was so depressing. I saw some just awful apartments. I was trying to keep my rent low." Eventually she did find a spot not far away. It was definitely a transitional space, and a big step down from the home she'd lived in for fifteen years, but it became her own haven. Soon Duff found an apartment just two streets away from the house.

They set up a duty roster of one week on, one week off. On Mondays, whoever had been on duty the preceding week would leave the house in the morning, and when the children came home from school that afternoon, the other parent would be there to assume his or her shift for the week. For the kids it was a series of relatively seamless transitions. Julia, a typically preoccupied teenager who was on the phone for most of her waking hours, found it quite comfortable. "For me the house never changed. I would never worry about who did the shopping because there was always food." The woman who had been Julia's and Ben's nanny was still there no matter whose week it was, and because she was there, the house always looked the same.

There were some moments, however, when the absence of one parent stood out in high relief. Julia remembers when she first got her period. "It was Dad's week. I was in the bathroom and I didn't want to explain it to him. My mom worked a lot at night ... so I was like, 'Where is my muuum?' Eventually I had to tell him because I couldn't get out of the washroom. I needed tampons and pads and he had to go out and get them for me." Having to tell her dad about something so personal was one thing, but Julia also resented missing out on a rite of passage that had become popular in her peer group. "I remember being mad because all my friends got period presents. Their moms would buy them some sort of gift or take them out, and I couldn't even find mine!"

The Monday handoff created a buffer between Esther and Duff, allowing them to avoid painful contact with each other and insulating the kids from the transitions. It became a routine with a comfortable rhythm for the kids. For Esther, though, having to leave her children was painful. "Every time I did it I cried. Every week back and forth, packing up my suitcase. Monday mornings were tough, but I realized that it was the right thing to do. It was the best option — short of staying together."

But Esther had a guilty secret, one that many divorced parents share but don't talk about freely. She found that she rather enjoyed having some autonomy. "I didn't always have the kids to take care of. Of course I called them every day, but I knew that I wasn't always responsible anymore. And that's part of what my burnout was — every day, every day, not even able to go to the bathroom by myself. So it was great to do whatever I wanted in my own place, little as it was. And as painful as it was Monday morning, by Monday night it was okay."

⁓

The arrangement lasted for four years. It wasn't perfect, but much of the strain was carried by the grownups. Esther remembered that it created a kind of displacement that even she, a seasoned traveler, found taxing. "Sometimes it was weird; no place felt like home. I felt like a nomad. At times it would be too much, and it felt like I didn't really belong anywhere."

Esther and Duff shared the costs of running the household. She was getting some child support, and she paid for clothes and other expenses out of that money. In settling their divorce, she ignored the advice of others and looked for a lawyer who wouldn't behave like a bulldog. "I'm sure that I didn't get the best deal, but it was enough for me. Why should I take money when I should be out there working and making my own? I realized that I just wanted what was fair, and that's what we did."

Part of the reason the arrangement was sustainable was that Esther and Duff remained flexible with each other despite their personal tensions, and the kids continued to come first. They helped each other out when necessary, if schedules had to change or children got sick. "I'd go back and spend the day with them if they were sick at home and Duff called me. I'd go because my time was still pretty flexible at that point. I could go to work whenever I wanted to, so I could still take care of them all day at the house if they needed something. If there were times he had to travel for work or whatever, then we'd switch and take two weeks at a time."

Another reason for the sustainability of the arrangement was a code of behavior that they honored between themselves. They never said anything bad about each other to the kids. Esther would protect Duff if the kids were impatient with him, and would try to support him in whatever he said or did. They attempted to be on the same wavelength and on the same path when they dealt with the kids, calling each other to ask, "Do you know that this is going on? What should we do?" And with

Julia, there were certainly problems they had to talk about and deal with together.

When Julia went into high school, she tested her parents in a way that only teenagers can. "I had a very big attitude. 'Nobody can talk to me, nobody can tell me anything.' I think it was just me going through normal teenage stuff." But Julia's hellion ways were not limited to having an annoying attitude. She got into a girl fight at one point and the girl pressed charges, so Julia had to go to juvenile court. "I remember first telling the story to my parents. My dad was mad and my mom was freaking out." Julia's sentence was probation for six months, which meant she had to check in with a probation officer. "I was a straight-A student with a part-time job and the lady looked at me and asked, 'What are you doing here? Do you think that the divorce of your parents caused you to rebel?' and I'm like, 'No. I was in the mall and my friends started arguing with some girl and before they knew it they were fighting. Do you think I sat at home and thought, Oh, my parents got divorced, I'm going to get back at them by getting in trouble? No, this is the last place I want to be.' After that the lady said, 'You know what, don't even bother coming here every month. Call us once a month just to let us know that you are not in trouble.' So I never went back to probation."

That encounter with the legal system jolted Julia enough that she dumped the friends she'd been hanging out with and straightened up. Esther and Duff had stood by her, spent a fortune on lawyers, and both had accompanied her to court. The importance of this support was not lost on Julia. "It's one thing when your parents are mad, but when they say they're disappointed in you, it's like, Oh man! I screwed up."

Ironically, although Esther and Duff were co-parenting well, the tension between them was still palpable, even to the children. Julia doesn't think her father has ever really overcome the disappointment or hurt of lost love. For that reason, she and her brother would try to avoid having her parents see each other. Julia observes that everybody in general is protective of her dad, who has remained single.

c⁓ɔ

Esther did meet someone else. A couple of years after she had split up with Duff, Michael came on the scene. She was careful about introducing him to the children and included him in their lives slowly. Once in a while he would have dinner and stay over at the house. He might drive them to school in the morning, so he just became another person in their lives.

Michael was the opposite of Duff in every way, and the children had very different reactions to him. Ben warmed to him right away. Julia saw him as an interloper and launched all-out war against him. She was very protective of her dad because he didn't have anybody new, and she treated Michael rudely, slamming the door in his face and ignoring anything he had to say. If he tried to tell her anything she would say, "Yeah, whatever. You're not my dad, don't talk to me."

Ben, on the other hand, enjoyed Michael's company, which further pushed Julia into a jealous snit. It really annoyed her that her brother was trading with the enemy. "They started spending a lot of time together. Michael would buy Ben hockey sticks and stuff. I would say that Michael was trying to buy Ben's affection and that it was easier to do because Ben was younger, and Michael couldn't pull that shit with me. I didn't understand why Ben was so attracted to hanging out with him. Now I see why. Michael is younger than my mom and he's very active and he's a cool person to hang out with. Now I see that, but at the time I didn't understand."

Over time, Michael's presence became a given. He waited out Julia's hostility. Ultimately she accepted him, but her resentment took a couple of years to recede. Now they get along famously. "I can't picture him not being in my life now that we get along so well. He just makes everybody comfortable."

Esther and Michael married, but relations between Duff and Michael, though civil, have never really warmed, a situation that Esther laments. "Communication is minimal. Once in a while we may have a long conversation, but it's still tense, after ten years. Probably if Duff had a partner, it would be a lot easier." Esther still believes that things could be more relaxed. "I could try, I could do it. I just feel he's still cold there, but that's his personality."

Julia understands why it might be difficult for her father to open up with Michael. "I don't think he really sees him as a friend. He sees him as his ex-wife's boyfriend or husband. For Michael it's not as hard because he didn't lose my mom to anybody, but I guess my dad felt that he lost my mom to Michael."

There may be a chasm between the adults as individuals, but as a family they have worked out ways of interacting around important events. Some family celebrations happen separately — which means the children observe some of them with their father's family and then with their mother's family — while others are observed jointly. "We'll have a Seder here and a Seder there and Hanukkah here and Hanukkah there," Julia explains, "but birthdays, because it's my day or Ben's day, that's when they come together. It's better if everybody comes to the same dinner. Sometimes after dinner on my birthday we'll go back to my mom's house for cake, and my dad will come and sit in the living room and have cake with my friends. It looks like he's tense — people have commented on it — and he won't speak until the end of the night. He'll stay for an hour or an hour and a half and then he'll get up and say, 'Okay Julia, I'm going to go.'"

A few other landmark events are observed by everyone together, but the kids know it's tough on their parents to spend too much time in each other's company so they move in, quietly, to try and ease the situation. "I won a scholarship, so there was a big award dinner and it was a black-tie event and my dad came and my mom and Michael came and we all sat at the same table." Julia's tactic for smoothing things out was simple but effective. "I always sit between my dad and my mom so that they're as far apart from each other as we can keep them."

In one instance a major event was celebrated separately and the character of the two events couldn't have been more different. Ben had two bar mitzvahs, one at his mom's synagogue and then one at his dad's. "After the one at my dad's," Julia says, "he had a lunch with his friends in some boring restaurant, and then we went to this huge monsoon party on my mom's side of the family where we all wore belly-dancing outfits. Everything was double."

With Michael's arrival, a new cultural tradition became part of the children's lives. "Michael's not Jewish, he's Irish-Catholic. We call him 'Bible Boy.' We were excited that Michael celebrates Christmas because now *we* celebrate Christmas and Hanukkah every year," continues Julia. "We have a Christmas tree, but it's not your normal Christmas tree. It's decorated with Jewish stars and real artifacts from Mexico and Belize and tropical fish ornaments. It's weird, but it's ours because it represents our family."

When Esther and Michael moved into their new home, the children were eleven and sixteen, and the "bird's nest" arrangement came to an end. Duff sold the family home and bought a new home close to Michael and Esther's. Julia chose to live with her dad full time, but can walk to her mother's house in five minutes. Ben goes back and forth weekly between his mother and father.

⁓

Ten years after the separation, Esther has few regrets. "I feel it's not normal for us to hook up with one person for the rest of our lives. We can't keep up that passion forever, which is what gets us in the trouble in the first place. You marry somebody at nineteen, what do you know? You're still growing up. *I'm* still growing up now, still changing and trying to get myself to a good place. It's fabulous if you do find the soul-mate connection and you're able to work through everything that happens to you in your life and still love each other to death. That's great, and it happens, but it's not normal that we stay with the same person forever." That said, she still has mixed feelings about the whole situation and how it affected her children, emotions that are common to many divorced parents. Even if the children say they're fine and tell you that you don't have to feel bad about what happened, Esther isn't sure that they really feel it deep down. "As much as they love Michael and everything else, and they know that I'm happier, I think that for them, if they had to choose, they would have left it as it was."

Julia doesn't look at it quite the same way her mother does. She sees that relationships come and go, which she accepts. She can't imagine her parents back together, and she isn't bitter about how her family has changed. "I don't look at it as if I don't have a family anymore; I have a family, we just don't live together. My mom is still my mom, my dad is still my dad. Sometimes when I go into someone else's home, it's almost weird to me. I think, 'You guys still do the whole mother/father thing, your parents still sleep in a bed together. Wow!' I think in the past people stayed together for the kids, but then people started to see that you can have kids and still have families without being miserable in your marriage. There are other ways to do things."

Julia hasn't lost faith in the idea of two people committing themselves to each other, but she brings a practical eye to the institution of marriage. "There are people who fight but they love each other enough to work it out and then there are people who just grow apart. If you really love somebody and that's who you want to spend the rest of your life with, by all means do that, if you can. I don't think marriage is an easy thing and I don't think people should expect it to be. I think they should expect it to be one of the hardest things in their life. I still want to get married and have kids and try to stay married as long as I possibly can."

When her parents split up, Julia had become part of a majority of her peers, but the way her parents dealt with it put her in the minority. Perhaps the kids in Julia's peer group understood, better than anyone, the value of a "bird's nest" arrangement. "When I told anybody about it they'd say, 'Oh, that's bizarre,' or 'That's different,' but then they'd *always* say, 'Oh, I guess that's good for you,' or 'Your parents really love you because they cared enough to go through that so that you guys didn't have to.' And that says a lot about the kind of parents they are."

CHAPTER THREE

Boomerang Breakup

"My heart had always gone out to every
kid who had to go back and forth and I knew
I couldn't bear making my kids do that."
— Darlene

TOM AND DARLENE were a mismatched pair from the outset. He's taciturn and emotionally closed; she's loquacious and emotive. Over the course of their marriage, which was often laced with tension, they floundered, separated, and regrouped several times. After a few false starts, they finally found a way to exit the marriage and enter into a new liaison that kept them close to each other and their kids. But it took patience, and ten years, to get there.

The couple now lives on a tiny island off the coast of British Columbia, where she's the local postmaster and he's a plumber and works on the ferries. They had migrated there seeking the bucolic life of a community removed from city bustle and the fast lane. Their home had magnificent mountain and ocean views, but the Arcadian setting was overshadowed by an ongoing dissonance between them.

The differences that plagued them had come into high relief when they decided to move to the West Coast and had gone there to do some house hunting. Darlene was pregnant with their second child, and the trip was so taxing that it was almost the end of them, she remembers. "The stress on our relationship was huge. When we came back to Ontario, Tom and I were hardly talking. I thought, 'We're in trouble, we're in *serious* trouble here.'" She was so mad at him that she threatened to exclude him from the delivery room. "He was not coming to my birth, thank you very much." They went into marital counseling, and it helped for a while. They decided to go ahead with the move, but they were never fully able to get onto secure ground with each other.

Within a few years, the balance between them became weighted toward their differences. Tom's need to keep his own counsel seemed like a poverty of emotion to Darlene, and she told Tom she wanted out. "I think feeling alone in a relationship is worse than being alone," she said ruefully. "I just felt like I was going crazy." Darlene knew she wanted to leave her husband, but her daughters were only four and nine. She was loathe to splinter her young family and she was determined that her children would not pay for their parents' inability to get along. They decided to try their own version of a "bird's nest" arrangement. It was a pragmatic decision as much as an idealistic one. At the time, it was the only way Darlene could figure out how to avoid moving the children from parent to parent. "We decided to let the girls have the house. This was my husband's and my mess. Why should *they* have to move?"

☙

The adults began shifting between households. It was a cobbled together arrangement that minimized disruption for the children, but it was difficult for the adults. "I moved in with a friend and my husband rented a cabin," said Darlene. "I'd stay [with my friend] one week and Tom would be in the house with the kids. The next week he'd stay in the cabin and I would be in the house with the kids." Being away from her daughters felt like harsh punishment to Darlene, but she was deeply committed to the idea that children should be raised by both parents and she didn't believe that children should live in two houses. "My heart had always gone out to every kid who had to go back and forth. To me it was completely and totally wrong, and I knew that I couldn't bear making my kids do that. So, it was the only thing I could come up with that felt fair for them. It didn't matter to Tom and me; nothing needed to be fair for us."

Their arrangement lasted for a year, but it was painful, and Darlene hated it. "It was absolutely horrible! I felt so sad when I had to leave the girls and my home at the end of my week. I have never felt so un-centered and unbalanced as I did during that year of our separation. Not having a constant 'nest' for that whole time seemed to make a bad situation unbearable. It was definitely one of the worst years of my life."

The arrangement didn't really suit Tom, either. He found it particularly problematic during the overlap times, and the change of command at the end of each week was stressful. "Although the situation did not work well for me personally," Tom said, "it made the girls' lives less traumatic and more bearable and that was the bottom line."

In spite of the minimal physical disruption for the children, it was still an emotionally unsettling time for their oldest daughter, Amberskye, who was quietly rattled by her parents' split-up. She, like her father, is very private, not given to sharing her emotions easily, so she struggled with it silently. Darlene remembers one situation that created confusion and embarrassed her daughter when they were on a school trip together. "Her class did a campout for three nights and one afternoon five little girls were all sitting in the tent and one of the girls looked around and said, 'Oh, everybody's parents are separated or divorced except for Amberskye's.' One of the other kids said 'Oh no, Amberskye's parents are separated,' and Amberskye froze like a rock. I tried to talk to her about it but she just couldn't." That memory is still difficult for Darlene.

Her children had always been the center of Darlene's life. From the moment she became a mother she began to organize life around putting the kids first. She took jobs that allowed her to be with them as much as possible. "As soon as I found out I was pregnant with Amberskye I went and got trained to drive a school bus. Back then we were allowed to take our kids on the bus with us, and Amberskye had the best social life of any kid I know. From the time she was four months old to the time she was five, I drove the school bus and she loved it."

Tom and Darlene made a deal to keep new relationships out of the family sphere. After they split, Tom had a girlfriend and the kids didn't know. One day when they were in town, the girls saw him coming down the street with this woman. "When I saw him, I thought, 'Oh, *shit*.' Later I said to him, 'Look, I don't care what you do in your private life away from the girls but don't you dare bring a woman to the house when it's your week in the house, that's totally not cool.' To me it just wasn't okay. He agreed and I still appreciate that."

After a year, though, the "birds' nest" arrangement became untenable for Darlene and she had to regroup. She told Tom it was killing her and that Amberskye was not doing well. "I said, 'This is crazy. We need to get back together.' So we got back together that Christmas, and things were okay for a while."

Darlene wasn't sure how Tom was feeling, but wanted to try to patch things up so she could be with her girls full time. "Tom is not good at being below surfaces," she says, "and maybe partly it's that he can't and partly that he doesn't want to — the reason doesn't matter." They wrestled with their communication problems by doing some self-help therapy with a book that provided exercises geared to mending torn relationships. "It was great," said Darlene. "It was hard for him, but he did it. It was ten weeks, and you were to give one

night a week to do these exercises. About six couples on the
island started to do this program, but Tom and I were the only
ones to complete it, and I'm sure it was hell for him. It was
okay for a while, but then you go back to your old habits."

⌁

Their reconciliation spanned ten years, but many of those
weren't very happy. The unhappiness found its way into the
family's daily life, and relations between Tom and Darlene
became prickly at best. Darlene began to lash out and Tom
retreated, and that infused the house with a nervous, uneasy
energy. Over time, their efforts to rebuild or even maintain
the marriage crumbled.

Annierose, the couple's younger daughter, couldn't figure
out *what* was off kilter in her home until she spent some time
in the company of another family. "I always thought that
every household had a bit of tension. It clicked for me one
day while at a friend's house. The parents were just so caring
and courteous of one another, I realized my parents can't be
that happy together."

Darlene was struggling with disappointment and her
inability to come to terms with her husband's nature. "You
know it's funny, even though I knew intellectually that Tom
couldn't demonstrate caring or that kind of thing, emotionally I just couldn't accept it. I couldn't deal with it. It hurt."
Looking back, Darlene realized that what had initially drawn
her to Tom was a sense that his quiet nature concealed a deep
thinker. They'd had fun together, and Darlene had been really

smitten with Tom. "I ended up thinking that I really wanted to be with this guy, totally ignoring the fact that I was doing all the talking and all the planning and whatever." Over the years, the feeling that they were ill-suited evolved from niggling doubt to full-blown frustration. "Tom is just incapable of showing love. I remember Annierose coming up to me when she was five or six, and saying, 'Why can't Daddy hug me? Why can't he cuddle me like you do?' And I just said, 'You know what, that's something that Dad doesn't do well and maybe that's something that you can give to Dad. You can teach him how to do that.' And she did." Whatever flaws there were in her marriage, Darlene made a point of differentiating those from her husband's strengths as a father. "He's been a great dad, he's been a wonderful dad, he would bend over backwards for his kids . . .[he's] always there for them."

☙

Darlene and Tom weren't ready to separate completely but they had to do something to change their status. As so many couples do before they're ready to take more drastic action, they made a change in their sleeping arrangements. It was a stop-gap measure to buy them time before confronting the underlying problem. It did relieve some of the pressure for Darlene, but not quite enough to lift the mood within the family. "That helped a lot . . . but it wasn't comfortable for Annierose. I think she felt the tension in the house. My fault was that I had become really bitter. I wish I had seen it, but I didn't get it at the time. I didn't really know what was wrong with me, I just knew it was pre-depression and I was silent a lot. I look back and I realize I was very uncomfortable to be around. I think they tiptoed around me and I feel really bad about that."

Darlene remembers one spectacular blowout she had, ostensibly about how the family had managed to accumulate too many possessions. "One day we were cleaning out the garage — an absolute nightmare. I knew I was angry but I didn't get what I was angry at. Things were piled on top of things, you couldn't get to the bottom, and I just went nuts. I was ranting about people in Third World countries making stuff so we could bury it in our garage, so that we could just go to the store and buy more so that they could get paid fifty cents a day so they could make more plastic. I was on a roll. And finally, the first time that anybody in my family had ever called me on my stuff, Amberskye said, 'Mom, why are you yelling at us?'"

Darlene just stopped in her tracks. She looked at Amberskye and said, "I'm not. It looks like I'm yelling at you, but I'm yelling at me." She couldn't believe she had allowed herself to do this. "I think that's why the rage was so strong. I said to her, 'I'm sorry, you're right. I'm just furious at myself for allowing this to happen.'"

Darlene's frustration had begun to affect the family's daily life. She wasn't managing well. Looking back, she still kicks herself for failing to see how her dissatisfaction was distorting the way she related to those closest to her. "I wish someone had called me on it early because it was releasing to be called on it and realize that this was not okay. You don't treat people this way." Tom remembers that the tension in the house during this period used to be so thick you could cut it with a knife.

Not long after that meltdown, the family began to downsize. Amberskye headed off to university, and over the next eighteen months Darlene allowed herself to envision some kind of reconfiguration of their family. The exercise of sorting out how to do it fell to Darlene, who had always been the family organizer. In the late fall, she approached Tom about the possibility of separating again. He wasn't ready to agree immediately, but given a few days to think about it, he said, "Yeah, we need to do this, this will be good." Tom says that Annierose and finances were the two things compelling him to stay near Darlene, but he could also see that he and Darlene needed to disentangle themselves from a relationship that wasn't doing much for either of them.

They began to imagine what shape their separation might assume. They were strapped for money, and real estate options are very limited on a small island, so their opportunities for choice were somewhat circumscribed. They owned a mobile home on an adjoining property, and Tom thought he might take up residence in that trailer. "He was going to move in the middle of January," said Darlene. "We had laid new floors and totally fixed it up, but about two weeks before he was supposed to move in, I thought, 'We can't afford to do this. I don't know how we are going to survive. I don't know how *he's* going to survive financially.' I spent about four hours sitting with the figures, but they weren't working." Darlene went to Tom and asked him if he could make the figures work. A couple of days later she asked, "Have you been able to figure out how to make this work financially?"

Tom said, "No."

In the meantime, Darlene had another idea. Some years before, Tom had built a small cottage next to their house, attached to it by a long, covered breezeway. It occurred to her that they could afford it if one of them lived there. She felt that in the long run it would be better for Annierose, and that they could re-address how to make it work financially to be on separate properties after Annierose left home. Tom liked the idea. The cottage, while tiny, has a living room, kitchen area, loft, and one bedroom. "Originally I was going to move into the cottage," Darlene remembers, "but then Tom said, 'Look, I'll move into the cottage, I don't really care,' and he doesn't. It worked."

Darlene believed this arrangement would be better for her daughter, who could sleep in the big house but move easily between her mother's and father's places. However, this wasn't immediately apparent to fifteen-year-old Annierose, who, in adjusting to the news that her parents were breaking up again, had fallen for the romantic idea of having two bedrooms of her own when her Dad moved to the trailer, and was disappointed at the news. Darlene sympathized, but felt that her daughter didn't have the experience to fully understand what living in two homes would mean. "She was going to want stuff that wasn't where she wanted it to be and, yes, it's only next door, but when it's pouring rain, which it does so much here, she's not going to want to leave to go and get it."

Things have played out much the way Darlene and Tom hoped they might. "Some weekend mornings Annierose will crawl out of bed, and still in her pajamas and with tousled hair and a yawn, go over to her dad's house and have breakfast with him," Darlene says. "She'll have lunch with whoever is home and in her opinion is having the best food. She will read a book and have a nap on either couch." Annierose likes that her parents live side by side, says Darlene. "Obviously she would rather us be together but that isn't the way it is. I think mostly she likes that we are so close."

Annierose herself had mixed feelings about her parents' split. She was relieved because they were happier and more relaxed, but "the hardest part was trying to evenly divide my time between the two houses," she remembers. "After some time, though, I found myself going from the peacekeeping role to making sure I spent an even [amount of] time at both parents' houses. I still preferred this arrangement a hundred times more than them living together."

It's impossible to avoid some pitfalls, though. There are moments when old irritants rise to the surface, prompting familiar behavior patterns, and this bothers Darlene, especially when it puts her child in the middle. "I must say, there are times when I'm pissed at myself because I don't keep my mouth shut," says Darlene, remembering when Tom, trying to work out some complicated transportation arrangements with his daughter, made decisions involving her car without consulting her about it. "He refuses to communicate with me and it just drives me crazy. So I said, 'Oh man, Annierose, I need you to tell me things because Dad doesn't tell me anything, and especially when you are talking about my car, you know?' And I just wished that I had shut my mouth."

Annierose hated being caught in the middle. It wasn't until she got older that she realized it wasn't her job as their child to try to fix her parents' problems. Darlene and Tom didn't have knock-down-drag-out fights, they were just tense with each other a lot of the time and the tension insinuated itself into Annierose's consciousness. "These weren't massive feelings, something that smacked you in the face. You never really noticed that they were there until someone else pointed it out."

Small annoyances aside, Tom and Darlene found simple ways of nurturing and maintaining convivial relations. The family created a new ritual where all three meet for dinner every Sunday. Tom and Darlene take turns cooking, so the venue for dinner switches back and forth. They rent a video or play games together, and Sunday has become the day of the week that's sacrosanct as family time.

❧

As Annierose reached the age where she too would be leaving the nest to head off to university, Darlene began looking to a future where it would just be her and Tom. Darlene is a planner, and she needed to find a vision that would inform the coming years. She said to Tom, "I'm thinking you might want to go to the mobile and live there, or I'll go in the mobile and you live in the house, but we need to figure out what we're doing. I need about six months' notice to get used to the idea, to plan, to figure out how it's all going to work, so think about it." A couple days later he announced that he was fine staying where he was. Darlene says, "It threw me. I said, 'You're going to stay in the cottage still?' and he said, 'Why not? It works and it's cheap.' I was totally thrown for a loop. I'm still not sure if I like the idea. In one way it ends up being handy, because the girls are going to be coming home to visit, and here we are, all in one place."

As time passes, Darlene has begun to see other threads that tie her to her ex-husband. "A friend asked me the other day if I missed saying to Tom, 'There's a big piece of wood that I can't chop' and I said, 'Oh, I ask him. We're still friends.'"

Tom and Darlene had reconfigured the family for the sake of their daughters, but sometime during their journey a new friendship began to take root between them, one that may survive long after there's a practical need for it to endure. They lean on each other in solving the problems of daily life, and that reliance shows itself in small gestures. "One day I realized the outside tap was on and I didn't know how to turn it off, so I got Tom to come and show me how to do it right. We're like neighbors who happen to share children — a cross between parents and neighbors."

The friendship's also there in more profound ways. "I know that I could ask Tom to do anything for me and he would do it," said Darlene. "And he could ask me to do anything for him and I would do it. I find that interesting, because even though we didn't work *together*, there's this bond that could never be severed."

CHAPTER FOUR

All in the Family

"It's not 'normal.' It's not what society
has come to believe happens between
two people who divorce."
— Megan

THERE WAS NOTHING EXTRAORDINARY about the way Megan and Mike's marriage fell apart. But the family they built after their divorce was *very* out of the ordinary.

They met when they were in their late twenties, at a party hosted by mutual friends. He was a military man stationed in Calgary and she worked in sales for a beauty products company in Saskatoon. Both were on the mend from bad first marriages, both were parents, and both had dealt with difficult divorces. Megan's husband had left her with no help and a daughter to raise on her own. Mike's marriage had ended in acrimony after his wife fell in love with one of his friends, and he had almost no contact with his three-year-old son.

Megan and Mike hit it off immediately and launched a whirlwind commuting courtship. Dating long-distance was tough on them, and after a few months Megan packed up her stuff and moved, with seven-year-old Amie in tow, to Calgary. She married Mike a year later. The following year their daughter Bethan was born and Mike was completely enchanted. He had missed his son's growing up and he wanted a baby girl to spoil and protect. "That was a happy time," he recalled. "She was born on my birthday. I couldn't stop doing the jig all day, all week, all month for that matter."

Mike and Megan had been married for about three years when the marriage began to sour. "There was no blame attached, no extramarital affair, just two people who were really incompatible trying to stay in a marriage that was not going anywhere," Megan remembers. "We didn't talk. We were together because we loved our daughter, and Mike was a very good stepdad to my daughter Amie, but there was no partnership there."

Mike was not an easy man to live with and he's open about his own role in the way that the marriage played out. "It was very hard, and I have to take much of the blame for that. I was probably drinking too much and partying too much and there were times that I couldn't stand myself. I had a really bad temper. I really can't blame her for wanting a divorce."

The tension between them was discernable even to Bethan, who was only a toddler but could see that her parents weren't getting along. "I can clearly remember when I knew that they started falling out of love, which would have been when I was three," she said. "I remember driving in a car once and they were having an argument and Mom kicked him out of the car and made him walk home." She also remembers disagreements that became more serious. "We were in our apartment and I heard this fight and I came running toward her to see what was wrong, and Dad was saying, 'I'm gettin' the hell out of here,' and Mom and I were crying together on the bed because of what happened."

On top of everything else, Mike had been wrestling with a depression that had taken a frightening and dangerous turn. He'd had a couple of nervous breakdowns and had become suicidal. The first time, he took an overdose of pills. "I didn't plan it. Bethan was in bed and Megan was out somewhere and I walked by the medicine cabinet and I just went for it — downed everything and lay down on the couch. When Megan came in later, I was breathing rather raggedly and she called a friend and they took me to the hospital. They pumped my stomach, and I ended up in the hospital for six weeks." The second time, Mike found himself wading into the Bow River, trying to drown himself. He snapped out of it long enough to get to the local hospital emergency room and ask for help.

Mike got himself back onto stable emotional ground and figured out how to manage himself in difficult situations. It was a long process, but he learned to control his temper. "I learned how to channel it. I still yell sometimes but it's not near to losing my temper." Mike has a wacky sense of humor and that helped them all during the rough patches, but underneath his kibitzing there always lingered a kind of melancholy.

"I like to make people laugh, and sometimes I use humor to cover up mad moods and depression. I get depressed and I get lonely. I don't always feel as funny as I act."

The marriage became hollow in a way that Megan couldn't fix and at a certain point she could no longer ignore it. "I think as women we long to feel that we're in a relationship where there's mutual respect and admiration, where there's room for each other to grow, where we don't feel hindered or held back by the other person." The marriage slid away slowly — no single angry explosion, no bitterness, just a series of incremental losses. "You wake up a whole bunch of mornings and think, 'Oooh, this might have been a mistake,' and then you have to do something about it. It was a slow realization that this was a good man, a good dad, but I didn't think I loved him anymore as a husband, as a partner, as someone I wanted to spend the rest of my time with. I loved him in a different way. I still love him to this day and I have no problem telling him that, and he still tells me that he loves me, but it was a different kind of love — one that you develop when you have a child together, a history."

Megan told Mike she wanted to end the marriage. He understood her feelings and agreed to move out, but not without indulging in a sulk. "I was still in the army and I moved back into the barracks. I didn't call or talk to Bethan for three weeks, and Megan finally got hold of me at work and said, 'You need to talk to your daughter. She misses her dad.' That's when I decided to snap out of it." He started visiting Bethan, going for supper and taking her out. "I'd put her on my shoulder and walk her five or six blocks to the corner store for a slurpy." Gradually a symmetry was established in the new arrangement. Mike lived nearby, saw the children regularly, and he says he and Megan got along better than they ever did when they were married.

⌁

The newfound ease even flowed through to the fomalization of their separation. It was a do-it-yourself deal, and Megan still laughs remembering it. "We went to a paralegal, did all the paperwork ourselves, went to court, and there were no lawyers involved, which was a great way to do it. I remember the paralegal saying, 'Why are you guys getting divorced?' because we were laughing when we were doing the paperwork. But I think it was a relief for both of us."

The divorce was a friendly one, but there were also hills and valleys. "You still have a lot of unfinished business, and as hard as you try to resolve those issues right away, it's difficult," says Megan. "I don't think we could have gotten divorced and continued to live under the same roof in the same house right away. We needed that space to adjust, and to grow a little bit as individuals."

For eighteen months Mike and Megan co-parented from separate homes. Then Mike decided to make a fresh start. He left the military and went back home to Nova Scotia, where his parents and siblings were living. "That move was devastating for him and devastating for me," recalls Megan. "I remember taking him to the airport and crying all the way there."

Compounding Megan's sadness was the guilt she felt as the one who had chosen to end the marriage. She worried that it was her fault Mike had decided to go back to Nova Scotia, and her fault that her daughter would be so far away from her dad. "He and Bethan missed each other terribly," Megan says. "They were very, very, very close."

Megan arranged for Bethan to go and visit her father. "I took her all over the place," Mike says, "kiddie places, and we just had a good time. She wasn't out of my sight for three weeks. It was sad taking her to the airport and letting her go. She was the last one on and *I* cried like a baby. I still get choked up just thinking about it."

Mike's sojourn in Nova Scotia lasted for over a year, until Megan was offered a new job that meant she had to travel a lot. Amie was in high school but Bethan was still quite young, and Megan wasn't confident that they were old enough to stay on their own. She had an idea. She phoned Mike and asked him if he'd ever thought of moving back West. "That one telephone call was all it took," she said. "Several weeks later Mike arrived back in Calgary and moved in with the girls and me." For Bethan, the decision was a no-brainer. "I remember Mom said to me one day, 'How would you feel if Dad came back?' Mom never said they were getting back together, just 'How would you feel if he came back and lived with us?' and I thought it was a fantastic idea at the time."

Mike became part of the household, ostensibly for six months until he could find a job and a place to live and get his feet under him. He had his own room, paid Megan room and board along with some child support for Bethan, and there was an easy rapport among everybody. "I was just glad to be around my daughter," says Mike. "Her school was only a ten-minute walk away and I wanted to walk her to school. At that time she still let me hold her hand, and it was good. It was good being around Amie, too." For Megan, it was like having a roommate or living with a brother. "There was nothing intimate or sexual between us at all, but it was great for him, for me, and for Bethan, who absolutely flourished because she had her dad back."

For Bethan, life was fine. It was calm, she had dinner with her parents most nights, and everyone looked after one another, so it felt like a normal family again. "I think that's what every kid wants. My parents always explained to me, 'It's not your fault,' because I think most kids in divorce feel that they did something wrong. They explained that they still loved me but that they didn't love each other anymore and that they were still really good friends. I think that's something that I carry even today — that they're really good friends and that they both wanted to raise me together."

As a couple, Mike and Megan didn't work very well, but they were really good at raising children — and sharing space. When they were not obliged to hold together a marriage, they were able to take pleasure in each other as friends. "He is an awesome dad. He's probably the funniest man I've ever met in my life — he cracks me up to this day. Bethan would come home at night or after school, could get up in the morning, and Dad was there." The arrangement made sense to Megan.

She had juggled the responsibilities of home and family life as a single parent and she didn't like it. "You're stretched and pulled, trying to keep a career going, trying to have a healthy home life. It was a benefit to all of us, financially, emotionally, to stay together."

୶

Over time, there were fewer and fewer compelling reasons for Mike to move into his own place. Megan could travel without worrying about her daughters, Mike was able to be an on-site dad, and the girls had two parents living with them. They did have to tolerate innuendoes and annoying jokes from some of their friends and acquaintances, though. People automatically assumed they were attempting reconciliation, and others made silly jokes that they must be having recreational sex if they were living under the same roof. Neither Megan nor Mike was particularly interested in dating other people, but neither was opposed to it either. Megan remembers being asked, several times, if she felt badly about going on a date when her ex-husband was at home. She would answer, "Well, no, why would I feel bad about that? I'd feel bad if I was going on a date and my husband was at home, but he's my ex, you know?" She often wished that people would recognize how much more work it took to live compatibly with a former spouse than it did to stay angry and bitter.

Megan and Mike were able to ignore the jabs and jocularity, but the situation was sometimes awkward for the girls. "Amie was in her teens, and I think there have been times where she might have been embarrassed by the living situation, and Bethan as well, because it's not 'normal,' it's not what society has come to believe happens between two people who divorce," says Megan. It was difficult for a little girl to understand why Mom and Dad were living under the same roof but were not together as a couple, and if Megan could change one thing, she would have made more of an effort to clarify the situation for Bethan from the start. She thought that her daughter would see that they had their own rooms and put two and two together, but that kind of math isn't always obvious for children, and sometimes it's hard to know how much to tell a child when a family is going through major transitions.

Megan knew things were on the right track, however, when she took Bethan to a six-week divorce support group where children met in one group and parents in another. "On the last night, the kids got to give the parents something that they had made. Bethan gave me a card that said, 'I'm glad that you and Daddy got divorced,' and I thought, 'Now you've got it!' She realized that we could both love her, but Mom and Dad didn't have to be married to do that."

Megan realizes that her situation with Mike was unique and her decision to co-habit with him would be inappropriate for many couples, "especially if there's bitterness and anger and the kids are stuck in the middle." But as far as she's concerned, the issue is not the arrangement; it's the underlying intention of their approach. "As parents and as adults, we have to learn to put our crap away and try to find ways — even

if they're untraditional — to make our kids' lives as easy and
as stress-free as possible."

꒰ᔔ꒱

Megan had another, very personal, motivation for wanting
to nurture Bethan's relationship with her father. Her own
parents had divorced when she was in her early teens, and it
was a deeply scarring experience. They had split up abruptly
after her father had an affair, and the entire divorce was
handled without explanation to Megan and her two sisters.
"That was a devastating time for my sisters and me. This would
have been in 1969 and we didn't know anybody whose parents
were divorced. We felt like social misfits."

Her dad never spoke to her about the separation. "I
remember my mom saying to me, 'How would you feel if your
dad goes to Edmonton and you and your sisters and I go to
Saskatoon and live where Nanny and Grampy are?' That was
it. That was the discussion. It might have lasted five more
minutes. I remember leaving the house — I was thirteen — and
I was absolutely destroyed."

Megan's father accompanied them when they moved. "My
dad and I drove in one car and my mom and my two sisters
drove in another. I remember feeling absolutely nauseated for
that seven-hour drive because I wanted to ask him questions,
but I was afraid to. We got to a hotel and I locked myself in
the bathroom thinking, 'If I stay in this room, my dad won't
leave. He won't leave without saying goodbye to me.' My sisters
and my mom were crying and I remember my dad knocking

on the door and saying, 'I have to leave, I have to leave,' and me refusing to come out. Finally, the knocking stopped and I heard the hotel room door close and I knew he was gone. I came tearing out of that bathroom and ran outside and just threw myself at him. That was the only time he talked to me about it, and he said, 'If you call me, you know I'm always there. If you write to me, I'll write you back.'"

The only address Megan and her sisters had for him was a post office box where they sent their letters. Despite all the secrecy, Megan was absolutely determined to find her father. "I ended up hitchhiking to Edmonton by myself three times before I could find out where my dad was. I remember getting there one time and phoning him. He came and took me right to the bus depot, put me back on a bus to Saskatoon, and said, 'If you want to come and visit me, you call me ahead and let me know that you're coming.' It was a terrible time."

These scalding memories spurred Megan to behave differently from her parents. Heartbreakingly, when her first marriage ended, her ex-husband was also not interested in being an involved father, although he lived only an hour or so away. There was no way Megan could cajole him into playing a role he wasn't prepared to take, and that grieved her, given her own history. "I knew what it was like to feel abandoned by one of my parents and I did not want my kids to experience that at all. Amie has often said to me that she felt very envious of Bethan when she was growing up because Bethan was a child who truly knew to the very core of her being that she was loved by both of her parents."

Remembering that her own parents never spoke badly about each other, Megan never spoke ill of Amie's father. She didn't want to color her daughter's impression of him, although she and Amie would laugh about his annual "bad dad" call every Christmas when he'd promise he was going to do better. Thanks in part to Megan's open-heartedness, however, Amie finally established contact with her estranged father in her late twenties, when he and Megan joined in celebrating their daughter's wedding. "Now it's wonderful," says Megan, "and I think he realizes that he missed a huge chunk of an absolutely wonderful young woman's life."

Mike had faced his own parenting disappointments and these informed his strong commitment to maintaining good relations with Megan. When his first marriage ended, his relations with his ex-wife, Margaret, had been testy. They were at odds about Mike's access to his son, JT, and the situation had disintegrated into a tangle of legal bickering. At one point, Mike wanted to visit his son, who lived in New Brunswick with Margaret and her new husband. They had been going to court to try to arrange the meeting, but the distance made the already difficult situation even worse. Finally Megan couldn't stand the tension it was creating and began to look for a solution. "Margaret had a lawyer, we had a lawyer and it was all this back-and-forth, back-and-forth, and nothing was being resolved at all. So I just decided to take the bull by the horns and I phoned her and said, 'This is ridiculous. He wants to see his son; I know you want him to see his son. Can't we work something out?' and an hour and a half later we had it all resolved on the phone, just the two of us. That was my first little foray into realizing that sometimes face-to-face dialogue, without lawyers, can be much more productive."

This inexpensive, simple resolution inaugurated a new period of cooperation between Mike and his ex-wife. When Margaret moved back to Calgary, the two families developed a close friendship — so close, in fact, that when Megan went into labor with Bethan, Amie went to stay with Margaret. "When I went back to work, Margaret actually provided childcare for Bethan, so JT and Bethan grew up knowing each other, which was perfect. Margaret had two other sons, and Bethan just figured we were all one big happy family."

Megan and Mike's new arrangement settled into a routine, and they lived comfortably together in Calgary for a couple of years. When a job became available in Saskatoon for Megan, she, Mike and Bethan (by this time Amie had moved out on her own) went together as a family. "Mike had been working as a baker, in a doughnut shop, and he knew that he would be able to get another job as a baker. I don't think it ever occurred to him that he wouldn't come, and it never occurred to me, either," Megan recalls, laughing.

ဇ္ဇာ

Two years after the move, this unusual family went through another shift that surprised even them. One cold winter night, Mike's brother Bill turned up on their doorstep, emotionally battered and reeling from a rancorous divorce in which his ex-wife had been awarded custody of their three young children.

"I was pretty much a shell of the guy you see before you, beaten down, depressed, and just literally needing a break," he says. Searching for solace, he had jumped in his car and pointed it in the direction of his older brother Mike, who lived halfway across the country with Megan.

The instant Bill set eyes on Megan he knew he had come to the right place. "She came down the stairs in her housecoat, and she looked at me, and the first words she said were, 'We've been expecting you.' It was one of the kindest things that was ever said to me," Bill remembers. Megan could see that her brother-in-law was fragile. "He was like a person whose life was so torn apart and shattered that if you touched him, he would break into a million pieces. He felt he had failed as a husband, as a man, as a father, with everything. He needed somebody to talk to."

Mike and Megan encouraged him to stay with them, and his visit stretched into a week, then a month, and then several. In the beginning, he and Megan hadn't known each other well, but he was family and she was a great listener. They spent many evenings sitting at the kitchen table or curled up on chairs in the living room, talking. "We talked for months," says Bill, "and in the process I was able to get myself out of the hole that I was in." He decided to stay, got a job, and began to think about how to rebuild his life. The little household absorbed him and they became a new family unit.

Then something happened that was completely unexpected. Bill and Megan fell in love. Megan remembers the dawning realization that she was becoming attracted to

Bill, and at first she thought, "'This really isn't going to go anywhere. He's on the rebound and I don't have the strength to help this guy heal,' but my God, I was attracted to him. And we had developed such an ability to communicate together. In the beginning, you're just two people having a conversation, and we talked about anything and everything under the sun. Time went on and it became more and more obvious that this feeling was definitely mutual. And then what do you do with it?"

It took Megan and Bill some time to get used to the idea themselves. They'd hold hands surreptitiously and sneak a kiss here and there. "It was a very slow thing to grow," Bill recalls, "and the whole time we were wondering, 'What would happen if Mike finds out? Will it change the dynamic of the way things are?'" The experience knocked Megan out of the comfortable groove as a single woman that she'd worked so conscientiously to find, and she felt incredibly guilty. "I had been on my own for five years at that time, and I was totally content with my life the way that it was. I wasn't on the prowl. And Bill was just coming out of such a bad situation. He wasn't looking for it either. But you know, sometimes the stars just align and it's hard to do something about it."

It was a challenge to find a way to become comfortable with what was happening. "I was truly convinced that I was losing my mind," says Megan. "I just couldn't see how any good could come of this. It was like being in high school again. We'd find excuses to go for drives together — it was like sneaking around. It didn't feel good to me and it didn't feel good to Bill. Honor and honesty are of the utmost importance to him." In the end, neither Megan nor Bill was able or willing to deny how they felt. They were so enamored of each other that, although it was a situation bound to be fraught with complications, they opted to build a life together.

As Megan and Bill were preparing to "go public" with their situation, Mike began to suspect that something was going on. There were a few flustered moments during evenings when they'd unwind in front of the television. "I remember thinking that they were getting awful cozy on the couch. I'd be sitting on some pillows on the floor and I'd hunker down and usually end up going to sleep. Every now and then I'd stretch and I'd see her hands move away and I said, 'Oh boy, something has happened here.'" Mike's reaction was one of avoidance. He didn't confront them but found himself ricocheting between conflicting emotions. "I wasn't too happy about it. I felt jealous, even though Megan and I weren't involved in any way. I thought, 'This is my *brother*, what the hell is she thinking??' I tried not to think about it much."

Denial eventually stopped working for Mike, and he lost his cool. "One night I had an argument with Bill or Megan and I went down to my favorite pub to get pickled. I made a phone call to Bill and he came down and we had a chat." At some point, Mike paused to consider what was at stake and asked himself a simple question: "Who am I to get in the way of their happiness?" He gave Bill his blessing that night, and agreed to try to make things work. Megan remembers the period of adjustment that followed. "In all honesty, and in all fairness to Mike, I think he felt a little betrayed. Certainly neither one of us ever intended for that to happen. I was not looking to fall in love with anybody, let alone my ex-husband's brother." In the end, it was more important to Mike to be close to Bethan than to succumb to his own hurt and jealousy, and so he adapted.

There was still the issue of telling Bethan, but as they wrestled with when and how to do it, happenstance took over. Bethan doesn't savor the memory. "I think the thing that bothered me most was that I found out about Bill and Mom before they told me. I was sleeping in my mom's room, and in the evening Mom was putting me to bed and said, 'I'm just going to go down and watch TV for a half an hour and I'll come right back.' I remember waking up at three or four o'clock in the morning and her not being there, and for some reason I walked right to my room and opened the door and saw them spooning in bed. I remember storming out of the room and bawling my eyes out. Mom said something like, 'We accidentally fell asleep together.' Even though I knew Mom and Dad were not together, I felt that Mom was cheating and what the hell was she doing in bed with my uncle?"

Megan winces at the memory. "Bethan was absolutely disgusted. She thought that this was the worst perverted situation that could ever happen. And I totally understood. I came home one night and there was a note from her on my bed that said, 'Either he goes or I go and I'm not leaving.' Bethan adored him as an uncle, but all of a sudden he was not her uncle anymore. He was the man that her mom wanted to spend time with. And he was her dad's brother. How sick was that?"

Bethan was devastated and confused. "I was angry, I think as angry as I've ever been. I felt betrayed and crushed and like somebody took my heart and just ripped it into a thousand pieces, but I don't know if things would have been different if they had told me when they were ready. That's the one memory that is the most hurtful. Every time I think back I still get angry inside."

Bethan wasn't the only family member who had a hard time with the way things were working out. "My mom had had a very difficult time with it," Megan says, grimacing at the memory of breaking the news to her mother. "I have such a strained relationship with her that I had to plan it all out. All she said to me was — in this voice that only my mom can use — 'Well, I *thought* you and Bill were becoming more than friends.' I was forty-one but I felt like I was twelve."

Bill's parents had a much different reaction. Surprisingly, Megan recalls, it was joyous news to a family that had always embraced her inclusion in their clan. "My father-in-law said, 'Good, now we get to keep her in the family.' They were delighted. I think they knew Bill needed something." But happy as they were, Bill's parents needed to scope out how their other son was handling this strange turn of events. They drove from Nova Scotia to Saskatoon to see everyone, and Megan understood their concern. "Mike was their oldest child, and I think they wanted to make sure, in their own minds, that he was okay with this, even though we had been divorced well over eight years by that time." The visit reassured them, and it drew everyone together. "We had a great time, Bill and I and Mike and Bethan and my in-laws."

❧

The arrangement held together, and the four continued to live under one roof. Best of all, Megan remembers, "Bethan eventually came around." Over time, Bethan adjusted, but it was challenging for a young teenager riding a hormone roller coaster, and she confided her feelings to her older sister. Amie helped her gain some insight, but Bethan admits that "to this day I'm still fairly wary about whom I tell that Bill is my uncle *and* my stepdad. I'm always afraid that they're going to think that it's incest, so I'm very careful. I'm afraid that they are going to judge me and think that my family is this trailer trash."

Bill was aware of how sensitive his niece was to appearances. "I always got the sense that through her teens she was a little embarrassed to bring anybody over to the house because it was a hard thing for her to explain to her friends that this is my dad and, well, this is Bill, he's my stepdad, or — the big joke — uncle-dad. When you stand back, it's quite comical. We've always tried to talk things over and to let her know that if she didn't want to tell anybody what was going on, that was fine. There are very subtle ways to tell people . . . they don't have to know that I have the same last name as her father, or that I'm his brother."

Megan and Mike were also careful about whom they

brought into their inner circle. Aside from a few raised eyebrows when people learned the details, most were remarkably tolerant. When all three adults found themselves in social situations, Mike's sense of humor acted as a leavening agent.

Now, as a young adult, Bethan acknowledges that though her family was different from most, she's quite comfortable with that distinction. "Who can say what a 'normal' family is anymore? I think the stereotypical family is not a man and a wife and their kids. The norm has changed and it has opened my eyes to being more accepting of things that deviate from what society might say is 'normal.' I never thought anything was wrong with our family; it was just a different family setup and it worked for us. For some other people, it probably wouldn't. I mean, I don't know how many brothers would be accepting of their ex-wife marrying their brother."

Bill was careful not to usurp Mike's role as father, and he took on more of a big-brother role with Bethan. "She had a father who adored her, a mother who loved her and worked well to provide for her, and there was me to go tobogganing and hiking and skiing with and to push her as far as the gym and stuff. It all worked out very well." When there were points of tension within the family, they tended to be around Bill's protectiveness of Megan. "The times I felt tension were when Mike and Megan would get into an argument. He'd raise his voice or point his finger, and I found I got quite annoyed and I'd stand up and we'd usually have words, and it'd be one of those situations where you'd think, 'Geez, one of us has got to go!' It wouldn't last very long, it's just like with any other sibling, you're going to get into a fight and then you're going to say, 'Aw, c'mon.' We worked through it, but it definitely made for some tense times."

❧

This family, which had already been transformed many times, was to undergo yet another alteration, one that would have challenged even the most mainstream domestic arrangement. Not long after Bill's arrival, Mike's ex-wife called to say she was having a lot of difficulties with their seventeen-year-old son, JT. He was in with a bad crowd, his mother explained, not going to school, and just going nowhere in a hurry.

Bill remembers the decision to bring JT to live with them. "He had gotten involved with drugs, he was being delinquent with school, had no motivation, was staying with a friend, and their way of making some coin was breaking into cars and stealing stereos or whatever was lying around. It was just not a good scene at all. We talked to Margaret about having him come stay with us. He needed a positive male role model."

So the family grew again, accommodating another character in need of guidance and support. JT had some serious growing up to do before he turned himself around. Mike, Megan, and Bill used to confer regularly about how to handle the wild thing that had come into their lives. "He was a typical young guy going through his teens, learning what his boundaries were, and growing up," Bill said. At times what he needed, according to Bill, was "tough love." "JT didn't want to respect a curfew, didn't want to give up smoking his dope, so we really had to come down hard on him. My brother is the complacent one when it comes to that." While Mike would deal with the problems by talking to JT and then hoping all would be fine, Bill felt that JT needed some consequences and believed that physical work was a good antidote for a young man's belligerence. "He doesn't want to come home at his curfew time? Living in Saskatoon, there's loads of snow, so go out and shovel the walkway in front of the seniors' complex. It was good. It taught him the value of respecting what limits he had, and it was physical activity to keep him out of trouble. Megan always referred to the house as the 'Bill Brown School for Bad Boys.'"

In Megan's view, it was all part of the process of raising kids. "JT stayed with us for two years and he really turned his life around." One of the highlights of his stay, Megan says, was his high school graduation. "They called him up on stage to receive a literary award, and we were just floored. Today he's twenty-five and an absolutely upstanding young man, and a huge amount of that credit goes to Bill. They were closer in age, and I think Bill could relate to his own youth and to what JT was going through."

ᙢᘗ

Oddly shaped though it was, the family unit survived for more than a decade. Once Amie and Bethan and JT had been launched into the world, Megan and Bill decided to move back to Nova Scotia. Bill's mother had died and his father was in failing health, and Bill was feeling a powerful pull to be near his own children, to build bridges with them if possible. Mike and Bethan stayed in Saskatoon for a short while and Megan believes that her daughter stayed in part to watch out for her father. "She's very protective of her dad, even to this day," Megan says. "Her dad wanted to stay where he was and I think she might have felt a little disloyal or a little concerned about how he would manage if she wasn't there. She still feels that bit of responsibility for him." Eventually Mike and Bethan decided to move to the East Coast as well.

The offspring of this family have moved on to worrying about other issues. Amie and Bethan are adults, which means there could be grandchildren someday. "We were trying to decide what the grandchildren would call Bill," says Megan. "I would be Nanny, and Mike would be Grampy, but what would Bill be? The girls have decided, if and when they have children, that Bill would be called Gruncle, because that's half uncle, half grandpa," she says and laughs.

How does the whole experience resonate, now that the household as it was has dissolved? Megan sums it up. "I think it would be a better world if all of us felt free to be loved by all of the people who love us — without any hesitation, without any feelings of betraying or letting somebody else down, especially with our kids. If we could just allow them to love the people that they want to love, and to be loved by the people that want to love them, without making them feel like they're torn or they're betraying somebody, that would be a perfect world."

CHAPTER FIVE

Forgive Us Our Trespasses

"I changed. I wanted more
adventure. She was strolling through
life and I was sprinting."

— Andrew

ALLISON WAS A NEW MOTHER when her husband, Andrew, dropped a bomb on their relationship. "When the baby was about six months old he told me that he wasn't happy. He said that he loved me but he wasn't *in* love with me." For Allison, the revelation was a complete shock.

Theirs had been a storybook romance. They'd been classmates in Grade Six, started dating in Grade Seven, and were almost inseparable by the time they were in their teens. Andrew was the football quarterback, and he thought Allison was the prettiest girl in high school. "She was my dream girl," he remembered.

Allison was raised in a comfortable middle-class suburb, while Andrew grew up in a block of apartments on "the wrong side of the tracks." She was the popular blonde; he was "the guy from the buildings that no one wanted to go near because they were kind of dangerous," according to Allison. They lived just a two-minute bike ride apart, but there was an enormous distance between their worlds.

Allison's was a "pretty average" traditional nuclear family, and she was comfortable with her place in it. "My brother was the smart one who went to university. I was more the princess who knew I'd be okay because I was pretty. I wasn't expected to go to university and I didn't — not that I couldn't have, it was just that they knew I'd get married."

Unlike Allison, Andrew had been raised in very challenging circumstances and nothing in his home fit the normal pattern of a family. "I lived with my father and my sister. My mother didn't live with us. She struggled with manic depression. There are lots of memories of not good stuff. It just wasn't a stable or enjoyable place to grow up." Andrew was twelve and his sister was ten when their parents divorced. The children remained with their father, and it was up to Andrew to fend for himself and look out for his sister. It was tough, and it left a permanent mark on his psyche. "If I could tell you one thing about my life that motivated me more than anything, it was my embarrassment about lack of money, clean clothes, proper food . . . not being able to bring a friend over." Andrew was determined he would emerge a different person from his parents.

Andrew was always at Allison's house when they began dating, and her parents grew very fond of him, virtually adopting him as their own. "He kind of lived in our basement," recalls Allison. "He calls my mom, 'Mom', and my dad, 'Dad.'" When they decided to marry, Andrew and Allison spent two years planning for the big event and he loved it. "We stockpiled, we shopped for mattresses, we shopped for dishes, and it was quite an exciting time. It was all a very fabled storybook beginning . . . childhood sweethearts, the old cliché." And after the fairytale wedding, their life began to unfold just the way Allison had dreamed it would. They had a dog, a bird, and then they had the baby. Andrew was becoming more and more successful in real estate, and Allison worked in a medical office.

But the plot took a twist that caught Allison completely off guard. According to Andrew, a distance had begun to develop between them even before the birth of their daughter. Allison was satisfied with the life they had built together, but Andrew was getting restive. "We started to have different interests. I would have separate activities with friends, things that we didn't do together. I remember Allison saying to me, 'You know, you should really act your age.' Act my age? I was twenty-nine or thirty-one, or whatever. I said, 'I *am* acting my age, you should act *your* age.' She just stayed in one position with her life. I developed a greater need to explore the world and do more things, where she was content."

Andrew had always been hyper-responsible and ambitious. He worked hard in his business life and pushed himself relentlessly to get his financial life in order. If he could work that out, he believed, everything else would fall into place. But, as he was discovering, he needed other things to be fulfilled. "I changed. I was a poor kid and I always thought that if I had money I'd be happy. As I started to climb up the ladder in the business world, I started to realize that I wanted more out of my life. I wanted more adventure, to travel and to do exciting things that I would never have dreamed that I would have the ability to do. She was strolling through life, and I was sprinting."

They tried marriage counseling for a while in an effort to resolve Andrew's dissatisfaction, but they weren't able to make much headway. The marriage was foundering, and finally it sank when Allison discovered there was another reason Andrew was so unsettled and unhappy. "He left and I found out that actually he'd been seeing a woman since I was I don't know how many months pregnant. It had started during my pregnancy, so that was the messy part."

She was devastated. "You know, I think I blocked a part of it out, but I remember moments of crying in the shower and having my daughter in the crib and just trying not to let her hear me cry. My mom was with me constantly, so she was a lifesaver."

❦

As Allison tried to re-establish some stability, Andrew was full of indecision. Over the next year he and Allison wrestled with what to do. They attempted to reconcile three times, but it never lasted. Though he cared for his wife and adored his baby, he was madly in love with another woman. Allison remembered it as a tumultuous period. "He was back and forth, back and forth for a while. He couldn't figure out what he wanted . . . he loved all of us . . . it was very hard."

Allison's challenge was to make sense of why her husband had chosen someone else. Andrew remembers that she blamed herself. "I said, 'It's not you, it's us. It's the togetherness of us. We're taking each other for granted, we just exist in life, we're just functioning in this marriage, but there's no soaring of the spirit. It's very dull, it's very flat.'" Allison worried about who would want her with a young baby. Andrew told her, "Allison, you're beautiful, you're gorgeous. I'm not going anywhere, there are not going to be any issues with all the things you hear about normally." But he says she was down on herself and that "she was very angry after that, understandably."

As a stay-at-home mother with a small baby, Allison was extremely vulnerable and it was a time of tremendous stress. Serendipity helped her to get some very important advice when a financial planner suggested she take a series of coaching and self-realization courses. She did, and found they helped her gain the confidence and skills she needed to sort out what she wanted from her husband for her daughter and herself. She began to exercise some control in a situation that had seemed to be out of her control. "After a while I realized I didn't want to be with someone who didn't love me. It wasn't like I was a victim. That gave me a lot of power when I realized that I had a say in what was going to go on. He tried to come back for all the good reasons, for the baby and for the marriage, but I knew *she* was still always in the background so that wasn't going to work for me. That's when things started to change for me."

Andrew, who had never lost the acute sense of shame about how he'd grown up, had tried hard to create his own ideal family. "I channeled that embarrassment into a lot of willpower and energy and drive about making a proper [life] — being there and participating in the birth and raising of a child, and giving her the best start possible, especially given the fact that I didn't have one. So that made it extremely difficult for me to say to Allison, 'This isn't working.' She acknowledged at the time that it wasn't working either. We both sat down and cried and said this is not at all what we had ever imagined we would have to do, or want to do, or should do, but it was a mutual agreement, ultimately." Failing in his marriage was a doubly wrenching experience for Andrew because he had so wanted to avoid his own parents' mistakes. "My entire fuel for success has been to do things much differently. I was a child from a divorce and it wasn't at all what I wanted. I had vowed that would never happen. That made it even more difficult to make the final decision . . . it was a heavy, emotional decision."

Their final parting happened during a weekend visit Andrew made to Allison's family cottage. "One of the defining moments in the story was actually our anniversary," Allison recounted. "We weren't together, we were separated. He was with Elizabeth, but he showed up at my parents' cottage. All of a sudden he was there and we were all like, 'Oh my God, Andrew's just walking through the door. What are *you* doing here?' We sat down outside on the porch that evening, and I guess everyone thought that we were getting together. We were talking for hours, but we were actually letting each other go, and we were deciding that together."

That weekend is etched in Andrew's memory, too. "I drove up to the cottage unannounced . . . I was usually the hit, cooking for the whole family and having a drink with her dad, hugging and kissing her mother. They were my family. Everyone was surprised to see me, including Allison. They all thought, 'He's home.' We sat outside and she knew and I knew. And I made a very strong commitment to her that no matter what, I was going to make sure that nothing bad happened to her."

༅

That's when the rebuilding began in earnest. During the year it had taken for them to resolve what to do about the marriage, things had been uncertain and painful for everyone. Now they could get on with creating a new life — one that worked for both of them. Andrew was true to his promise that he would support Allison in raising their daughter. Allison stayed in their house for several years, and he continued to commute between his new home and Allison's. "I was up there three nights a week when AJ was a six-month-old baby. I told Allison to go to the gym, go see her friends, go to dinner, all the things you would normally do." Andrew's friends told him that he was with his child more than they were with theirs, and they were full-time dads. Andrew was building his career, starting at six o'clock in the morning, working until six at night, driving from Toronto to Allison's in Aurora, staying until eleven o'clock, then coming home. "It was killing me, the physical timing and the energy of it."

Allison, meanwhile, had made a remarkable decision about how to deal with Andrew after her discovery of his affair, and their breakup. She credits the coaching sessions for this. "I became committed to being co-parents who loved each other no matter what. After all the time that Andrew and I had known each other and all the history, I wanted the love to still be there, but a different kind of love. I wasn't attracted, it wasn't about that. It was a human-to-human kind of love. I wasn't committed to my daughter having anything less than what she would have had if we were together. I mean her life was going to change, but she was only six months old.

"I think I got more clear about commitment, the word commitment even, through the coaching. I remember in one of the courses I was writing a letter as part of our assignment. I stood up and read something like, 'I forgive you for breaking up our family, and da-da-da.' The leader said, 'You know what, just go back and re-write your letter. You haven't forgiven him one bit.' So that's when a light bulb went on in my head. I thought, 'Okay, I've been blaming him. I'm still making him wrong, blaming him.' So I finally gave that up, because I know for sure that to have what you want, there's always something to give up. I can still go back to what I went through, what he did, but I played a role in that. People just make their 'exes' wrong and they don't take responsibility for what happened on their part."

❧

The first year of Andrew's and Allison's separation was also difficult for the woman Andrew had fallen in love with. Elizabeth, who was single, unencumbered, and three years younger than Andrew, was buffeted by the turbulence in his life. She became involved in a kind of chaos and she was unable to extricate herself. "Your heart can sometimes lead you instead of your brain. Unfortunately, the circumstances weren't great, but the relationship was amazing and it was worth everything that we had to go through to be together. In the end it worked out, but it was a long road. A long road."

Elizabeth had to deal with being "the other woman," and the cliché of "the other woman," but she admits she learned a lot about herself. "Life takes you places, and I don't know, it's almost like a journey of learning, and I had to learn the hard way."

It's not easy for her to talk about this part of her life. She doesn't share it readily, and is wary about being judged harshly and blamed for ruining Andrew's marriage. Looking back on the early days of her romance isn't something she does with much fondness. "Yes, we had great times together, but there were a lot of upsets, you know, a lot of torment about what to do, what not to do; a lot of hard choices, for him, for me, for Allison. I was somebody who didn't have — if you want to look at it this way — baggage. I could walk away and I chose not to. That was a hard decision, that was a big decision."

Why did she stay? Most affairs end in disaster. Andrew never wavered about his commitment to his daughter and Elizabeth always knew that whatever relationship she chose to have with Andrew, his ex-wife and daughter would be part of the picture. "I felt that we connected at such a level that I didn't really have a choice. I knew that he was good for me and would help me grow into the person I wanted to be and could be." Ironically, one of the things that endeared Andrew to Elizabeth was the fact that he struggled so hard to make a decision and to extract himself from a quagmire of doubt and self-recrimination. "It's not like he didn't care and said, 'I'm going to be with Elizabeth.' He went back and forth three or four times, so tormented in what to do. Even today, if he talks about it, he'll cry, because he still feels so much guilt. He's someone who really cares, genuinely loves and cares. I don't think all men are like that. I loved him so much . . . I wasn't going to let the work hold me back."

Elizabeth made the commitment to stay with the relationship, as did Andrew. However, being between two families, especially when they were a forty-five minute drive apart, took its toll. "It was tough. I was working a lot, just building my business," Andrew said. "One hundred percent commission . . . if I wasn't making a deal, I wasn't getting paid." On top of the stress of business and parenting from a distance, Andrew was trying to "cultivate a relationship that had started in the eye of a hurricane." He remembers the impact of that time. "It aged me, no question about it, really aged me. My resiliency was definitely compressed. I had a crushing amount of guilt that I was disrupting not only myself, not only my wife, but also an innocent baby. So I was very, very hard on myself."

The arrangement between Andrew and Elizabeth and Allison began with a fairly typical shape. From very early on, Allison had the baby most of the time, while Andrew spent two evenings a week with AJ and took her to be with him every other weekend. Andrew remembers that this was a kind of baseline to their agreement. "It was a strong commitment not to be a stereotypical 'bust-up' husband and wife. Financially, I gave more than I needed to give. I definitely gave the time and the freedom for her not to be tied down to a young baby."

There was some tension around Allison's relationship with Elizabeth, and they kept their distance for the first while. On Andrew's weekends with AJ, he would pick her up on Friday and then Allison would come for her on the Sunday. "Because I knew Elizabeth was living with him, he would meet me in the lobby," Allison says. "I didn't want to talk to her, I didn't want to know who she was. This is when it was pretty messy, so he would just meet me in the lobby with the dog. We had an English bulldog at the time, so the dog, the kid, everyone went together."

❧

Eventually things began to thaw between Allison and Elizabeth. They were slowly beginning to build their own relationship, but there was a reckoning. It was an encounter that everyone remembers as being difficult and full of tears. Allison invited Elizabeth to have coffee with her, just the two of them. Allison had had some coaching around how to handle the situation, and had planned what she wanted to say and the questions she needed to ask. "She wanted to meet me for coffee," Elizabeth recalls. "She said, 'We'll talk — it'll be a good conversation. We'll talk about where we want to go and everything.' But we went for coffee and she laid right into me. 'How could you do that, what kind of person are you?'" Elizabeth felt ambushed.

"I felt that it was a total personal attack and I think that's what her intention was. I had gone to meet her under a completely different premise; obviously I wouldn't have met her for that. It was at that point I told her if she had something to say, to tell me when she was going to say it, not to lead me somewhere to pretend we're going to be friends and then lay into me. Of course she's going to have feelings of anger and everything. I don't blame her for that." Andrew made a phone call to Allison right away, to say enough was enough. Elizabeth says, "he basically picked up the phone and said, 'What the hell was that?'"

Fortunately, the encounter acted as a catalyst to bring the women to a better understanding of each other. "It turned out that it was probably the best thing that could have happened," remembers Allison, "because a few weeks after that Elizabeth wrote me a letter saying that she'd never meant to hurt me, and she would never take my place as AJ's mom. It was a nice letter, so we started to work together after that a little bit better."

The confrontation led to a ceasefire, and eventually to a peace agreement. Elizabeth, once she calmed down, understood Allison's need to vent. "I think that at that time she just needed to get it out, and she got it out. You know, I probably needed to hear it. I had to work through all of that stuff on my own anyway. Regardless of Allison actually saying the words, I felt it all, so it wasn't news to me. Could I have taken that and been super-angry and resentful of her for the rest of the time? Sure, I could have, but was that going to help me in my life and building my life with Andrew? No it wasn't. We really needed to get past that stuff. It's all about what's going to make it work. It's all about clear communication."

༄

It's one thing to believe in communicating, but another to commit to it everyday, especially when there have been so many hurt feelings and disappointments. Anger can hover in the shadows, making an unexpected appearance during tense moments. In the aftermath of a ruptured marriage, behaving well in everyday life can take a prodigious effort. Allison broached the idea to Andrew of enrolling in the coaching courses she was taking. She had learned how to manage complicated and toxic emotions, so why wouldn't those skills benefit Andrew too? "She asked me if I would do it, on my own, and in one split second I said, 'Absolutely.' I encouraged Elizabeth to do it with me too, because if this was as powerful as it seemed, I wanted all the people in my life to benefit. We did it and that was a major bridge-building exercise because we could communicate openly and freely about how we felt."

Allison remembers how pleased Andrew was about the effect the courses were having on the way they all interacted. "He loved it because it was great for him. He loved having Elizabeth and me be friends, and all of us working together made it a lot easier for him."

Everyone's relationships were going through a rebalancing, a kind of normalization process, which Allison cherished. "It was better that we all get along and that my daughter have more people loving her. That was how I looked at it." She and Elizabeth were in complete agreement about the importance of keeping these priorities straight. "The single leading factor in making the whole thing work is that we've put AJ's best interests first," says Elizabeth. "When you see this little child you can't help but do that. You can't help but make that decision."

The process took Elizabeth to a place of some personal discomfort. Allison remembers this with empathy. "She was not a bad person, she was a nice person, and she did the courses and went through a lot. She would call me and apologize, in tears. She had to really forgive herself for what she thought she had done that was really wrong. And the interesting thing for her was that there was a background of that with her parents."

When Elizabeth was fourteen, her father had left her mother for a younger woman. Her mother was crushed, and leaned heavily on Elizabeth for support. "It was a typical European family where my mother did everything — cleaned, stayed home, took care of four kids. My dad worked all day, would come home late, eat in front of the TV while the rest [of us] were at the table. He grew up in a time of war, was sent to some concentration camps — he was Polish — and he would get abusive sometimes with my mother.

"They weren't happy for a long time. Actually, when he left, I was so happy he was gone. It was that bad, that all of us were, 'Yes, okay, it's devastating that he's left my mother because my mother's alone, but thank God he's gone. The fighting will stop, the hitting will stop, all of that craziness will stop.' I resented my dad for a long time. I don't any more; I've gotten over that. And I think that being involved in an affair myself helped me to grow through a lot of the anger or resentment."

The coaching courses helped Elizabeth to understand that her discomfort stemmed from more than having betrayed Allison. "I always felt better after Allison said, 'I forgive you,' but it wasn't until I talked to my mother that I finally got it. Here I was 'the other woman' in this relationship with Andrew and it was 'the other woman' who had destroyed her life when she was married to my father. So it wasn't until I sat down with my mom and said, 'I'm so sorry, I can't imagine how you felt when I did this.'" Even the memory of this moment is emotional for Elizabeth. "It wasn't until my mother forgave me that I felt like, 'I'm okay, I'm not a horrible person,' but it wasn't until I had both of them forgive me. And I had to take responsibility, I couldn't just duck my head into the sand and pretend it wasn't my fault."

⸎

As the new family triad began to figure out how to set things up for the longer term, they decided to sell the house Andrew and Allison had owned in Aurora and buy two affordable houses close to each other in Markham. Andrew knew a developer who helped them find homes that were just twelve doors apart. When Allison moved in, Andrew pitched in and set up her closet organizers, hung her shelves, and arranged to have her air conditioning installed.

Eventually they shared time equally with AJ, who flour-ished. There was a lot of overlap between the two homes, and schedules and boundaries were remarkably flexible. Allison remembered that "AJ loved it. I think there were moments when she'd want her dad or she'd want her mom, but we never kept it strict. When she was with either of us, we could come over at any time. If she was at her dad's house and had the flu, I'd sleep over, we'd be together. He'd come over if she had the flu at my place. We were parents who still parented together no matter where she was. We had keys to each other's homes. If I was home and Andrew and Elizabeth got stuck, couldn't take her to school one morning or couldn't pick her up, they'd ask me, and I'd make requests of them if I needed help. So it was always a back and forth, everyone helped each other out."

Living close to each other has been one of the keys to the success of their arrangement, which Elizabeth describes in terms of how if affected AJ. "If she came home today and said, 'I want to go to Mommy's,' I'd call over to Al's, we'd go outside, Allison would wave down there, I'd wave, and AJ would walk. She can do that anytime she wants. I wouldn't say, 'No, you're not going over to Mommy's.' We're so open about that kind of stuff, whatever she needs, she knows that she has a secure environment and that her family loves her."

Elizabeth and Allison began to do the coordinating over AJ's schedule, and Elizabeth designed a binder system that contained information about the details of AJ's life. It traveled between homes and helped everyone keep track of birthday party invitations and library books.

For AJ, this family with an odd shape made complete sense. Allison smiles as she describes her daughter's comfort with a situation that had taken such measured control to craft. "She just grew up with it, Daddy and Elizabeth and Elizabeth's mom and me. That was just her family. Whenever she drew pictures of her family at school, it was always all of us and the dog."

In the life of every family, there are watershed moments, and sometimes they happen in the most unexpected venue. One major rapprochement took place at a birthday party Allison held for AJ. After the separation, Allison's parents, particularly her father, had been quite hostile toward Elizabeth, although they had never met. It was AJ's second birthday since the separation, and Allison felt it was time everyone met. She invited her family, and Elizabeth, to attend the party. Elizabeth agreed to go. "I remember meeting Allison's family for the first time . . . it was awkward. It was terrifying to go, but I think I just decided I was going to be myself and whatever was going to happen was going to happen."

Allison had to run some interference to get everybody to attend. "My dad was still pretty angry. He said he wasn't coming to the party, 'not if *she's* going to be there.' But he came. He saw that we were okay together and how we were working together, this kind of new family, friends."

Elizabeth recalls that she helped out a lot. "I played with the kids, and I think they saw that I was just a good person, and they could see that AJ interacted well with me and that she was going to be okay. So they decided that they were going to let me into the extended family. They didn't have to."

Allison had created an environment where her father was able to soften, and change his attitude toward Elizabeth. It was a poignant illustration of how people's opinions can shift given the right opportunity. "He kissed her as he was leaving. It's amazing how, when you're a certain way about something, you can inspire other people. That's when we really started to bond and become this extended family."

Andrew, who had maintained an ongoing relationship with Allison's family, noticed that the birthday party had a lasting effect on the relationship between Elizabeth and Allison's father. "Every single time he sees her, he will not enter the room where she is without kissing her on the cheek, and will not leave the room without kissing her on the cheek."

For Elizabeth, that gesture had enormous significance. "Her father hugged me. I can't remember what he said, but he said something, and just the motion of the hug, I knew that I was accepted. It was a great moment. You come out of an affair thinking that you're a horrible person and then you have to really build a case as to why you're not. All you can think of is negative. It was validating for me when her family accepted me."

༄

When AJ was about three years old, a new man, Kurt, came into Allison's life. They were in a leadership program together before they ever dated, so Kurt had heard Allison's story. When they did begin dating, they quickly became serious and after a short courtship, they decided to marry.

Kurt's personality was completely different from Andrew's. "Andrew's a salesman, Kurt's not. Kurt hates sales. Kurt can be in your face with his military background and that doesn't work for Andrew," Allison explains. But that didn't stop them from making an effort to connect with each other. "They're different people. They'd never be best friends if we weren't in this situation, but they make it work."

The introduction of a new character to the mix necessitated some tinkering with the balance of the arrangement. "Every time I was dating someone new or had a new boyfriend, Andrew was always there in the background, asking 'How's it going?'" Allison laughed. "I had to create more boundaries after I was married, because Andrew was used to kind of taking care of me or helping me."

Andrew talked about how he and Allison had become like

sibling confidantes. "I was never once jealous, which told me that my heart and my soul had left the relationship. I had been jealous a tremendous amount when we were teenage kids and in our twenties. When I went up to see AJ during the week, when she was still a toddler, Allison and I would have a tea, have a beer . . . and I'd ask her, 'What's happening, how are you doing, how's work?' We'd talk about her dates. I was her fatherly, brotherly, friend figure more than I was her ex-husband."

Over the years the two couples have maintained cordial relations. Andrew explains that they enjoy each other's company, which benefits his daughter. "Every time we have AJ in our home for the week or two weeks, Kurt and Allison will come for dinner once during the week, usually on a Wednesday, and we'll have a couple of bottles of wine and honestly have a good time. I started it because I wanted AJ to see that even though her parents chose to not live together, we were all still a cohesive unit. I wanted to give her a sense of family, a sense of belonging, a sense of comfort. I didn't want her to be a nuclear thing that gets shuffled between two bases. That was the motivation. And we're going to keep doing it."

There was one major disagreement between the men, which erupted one night over dinner at Andrew's and Elizabeth's. Something Andrew said ticked Kurt off, and he stormed out of the house. The women stayed out of it, and waited for the men to sort it out on their own. Andrew made the first conciliatory move and called Kurt three weeks later. "I said, 'Kurt, we need to talk.' He goes, 'Yeah, I've been meaning to call you.' And you know, we were just two school kids in the schoolyard pushing each other around. He's not a very communicative cat. He didn't apologize, so I just took the conversation and looked for the goodness in it. Since then we're back to where we were before."

⤫

Both couples have married, and attended each other's weddings. They each have new babies who were born at almost the same time. And lately, the two families have even traveled together. Andrew came up with the idea, and while some of their friends and family find it weird, it makes sense to them. Allison explained it this way. "Built-in baby-sitters. AJ gets her vacation, we get a vacation. We go out and they can baby-sit, they go out and we baby-sit. It kind of worked for everybody, that's how it evolved."

Elizabeth remembers arrangements they made for one trip. "We all stayed in the same condo. It was two bedrooms with a pullout couch and we shared a kitchen, but we're that comfortable in our relationships that that was fine. Because I see Allison as a friend, I don't mind traveling with her. It's fun, we'll have great chats; it's not necessarily a chore when we go on holidays."

Just the fact that these couples travel together is remarkable in itself, but it has also had another completely unexpected ripple effect, according to Elizabeth. "I think that it's helped other people to grow a little bit, too. My mother actually came to Christmas at my dad's where my dad hosted it with his wife.

My whole family was going to be there and I said, 'Dad, really, can't you just invite Mom? To leave her out, she's going to be sitting home by herself . . . ' and he called her up. She came and they were very friendly with each other. My mom and my stepmom can actually interact now, and they never had that before."

Andrew wants AJ to grow up with the sense that she lives in an extended family, an idea everyone has embraced. In addition to ferrying both families off to vacation spots, efforts are made to create a sense of extended family within the home, Elizabeth explained. "The fact that we travel together is normal to AJ. We have family dinners, it's normal to her. I'm trying to help grow her confidence and self-esteem, so once a week now she's helping to make dinner. She gets to choose the menu and she has to tell me what ingredients she wants and I buy them. This week we invited Mommy to come. Grandma was visiting, so Grandma came too. To AJ, it's totally normal. We could be over at her mom's place for dinner and no big deal . . . whereas maybe in other families it's a big deal if daddy and the stepmom are coming for dinner or the other way round. But here it's just the way it's always been."

As if everyone's lives weren't complicated enough already, another wrinkle appeared in the arrangement. Kurt was offered a job in Winnipeg, and since jobs in his area of expertise are hard to come by, he took it. He and Allison consulted Elizabeth and Andrew, and then began to organize themselves to maintain a commuter marriage. AJ stays in Markham, and Allison and Kurt travel to be with each other and their new baby. Kurt is home ten days a month, and Allison is in Winnipeg ten days a month with the baby. They have an apartment there, and are together every weekend. Elizabeth and Andrew have been supportive of this and have switched to a two week on, two week off schedule with AJ to facilitate the arrangement.

Allison is living a life she couldn't have imagined as a teenager growing up in the suburbs. "It's not the white-picket fence, but it's exciting. You know, everything pushes me. When Andrew and I broke up, I was pushed and I grew in a certain way. I lived alone with a baby, it just pushed me to another level. And sometimes I'll think, 'I'm alone with the baby now.' It's almost like being a single mom at times. Maybe what happened with Andrew and me set me up for this, like I got trained."

And at the center of it all is a little girl who has never been forgotten. She is why all these adults have compromised and cooperated and sacrificed. She's the reason for all of their efforts, according to Andrew. "I want AJ to have as normal a childhood as possible, and I want her to see her parents happy. We always pose for a picture with the three of us, all seasons. She sees me hug and kiss her mom on the cheek, and I've told her, now that she's old enough — she's going to be nine — 'Daddy and Mommy love each other tremendously. Tremendously. And Daddy will do anything for Mommy. We don't live together, we're not married, but I want you to know that the two people that made you are very, very tight with one another."

CHAPTER SIX

Domestic Détente

To a lot of guys, I didn't have
the balls to leave. A lot of women think
I had the balls to stay."
— Allan

WHEN ALLAN AND MARIA got married, their friends saw them as a model of matrimonial bliss. They'd met in a faraway place, had a long-distance love affair that spanned several cities, decided to build a life together, and produced three wonderful children. But when the love affair ended, their separation was anything *but* an example of model behavior.

Their marriage did not drift into stasis. It disintegrated, big time. As it did, the mood between them was corrosive and their interactions filled with animosity, their frequent fights coming dangerously close to blows at one point. But somehow, for the sake of their children, they pulled themselves back from the brink of all-out war and slowly found ways to reshape the family. It was an effort driven not by altruism but by bloody-minded tenacity, and the outcome was a precarious truce that Allan compares to life in a demilitarized zone. "We have a peace treaty, for sure, but I'm not a dummy and I know that most of the time when people separate or divorce, the kids go with the mom and the dad gets them once every two weeks or every second weekend, and I couldn't agree to that. Why the hell should I get my kids once every two weekends when *she* bailed on *me*?"

This is the account of a fragile peace, a reconfiguration that could just have easily have gone in the direction of post-marital nightmare. What is noteworthy about this family's story is that the nightmare didn't happen.

❧

Allan and Maria have been estranged as intimate partners for more than a decade, but they still share a duplexed house with their three young daughters in an affluent downtown Montréal neighborhood. They've been able to co-parent their children — successfully — since their relationship fell apart, but have never been able to transcend their own disagreements or find any real harmony with each other. Logistically they have a setup that works well for the family; emotionally, the jury is still out.

Just looking at Allan and Maria you can see how different they are. She is tiny, with dark hair, perfect white teeth, and a luminous smile. She's warm and sunny, and radiates calm. Allan is slight and balding, with intense blue eyes and delicate, carefully manicured hands. He's somewhat standoffish, and projects a restlessness he doesn't quite know what to do with.

It was Maria who chose to end the marriage. Her relationship with Allan had begun to founder shortly after they wed. Their first baby came along within a year, and the second arrived a little more than fourteen months after that. With two small children, Allan and Maria were consumed by running and raising their family and somewhere along the way their own relationship got lost. Maria had become emotionally numb and reached a point where she had to do something about it. "I kept telling Allan, 'I'm sorry, I don't feel anything anymore,' although I *did* feel something — anger, anguish, I don't know what."

Allan was not ready to give up on the marriage, and dealing with its end was not easy for him. He still bristles about it, and his words are bitter when he speaks of Maria. He remembers that the first signs of discord began to appear sometime between the births of their second and third daughters. "Between Olivia and Michela something clicked in Maria. Somehow she saw me in a different light and at a certain point, I just couldn't make her happy anymore. That was extremely frustrating for me, because I couldn't understand why. We were *both* extremely frustrated, yet unable to talk to each other about it, so there was this impossible situation. I think that I stayed in love with her longer — at least I maintained the trappings of a marriage — longer than she did."

Allan wanted to make the relationship work and Maria said she didn't know if they could rekindle anything, but they could try. "We did go to see a marriage counsellor and had a few sessions with her," Maria says. "Those helped us to deal with each other so that we would be more civil, but it did not bring back the relationship." Counseling helped Allan, too, although not in the way he had hoped. "It was bullshit, in the sense that it was way too late to make a difference . . . at least we talked to each other and said things to each other that we never said before. Apart from that, our ability to talk about what we're going through is not that great. I think part of the reason is that the rawness is still there so it's really hard."

What Maria regrets is that she bottled up what she was feeling. "One of the biggest mistakes Allan and I made was that we didn't communicate the things we felt at the time that they were happening. I kept lots in, and that built resentments and one thing stacked on top of another." Allan agrees, and while he held onto hope that the marriage might survive, now he's fairly realistic about how things turned out. "I really think that the fundamental problems that Maria and I have would have existed with or without kids. You have two very independent, hard-headed people, both of whom wanted to run the show and neither of whom was willing to give in to the other. So how can that work?"

Well, it didn't work. When they fought there was little room for conciliation, according to Allan. "Maria would say, 'If you don't like it, why don't you get out of here? Why don't you just leave?' and I would say, 'Why the hell should *I* leave? I'm not going to leave, you leave.' I think the only reason we are in the situation we are today is because we are both too stubborn to go." But there was one compelling reason that Allan stayed close to Maria: he did not want to lose his children. He was fierce about his right to maintain full access to them, and that stoked his resolve.

☙

Neither Allan nor Maria had any intention of being a part-time parent. They could have fought each other for custody of their children, but they avoided doing that. Allan believes that children always suffer when their parents split up, and he reluctantly concluded that he and Maria would have to continue living close to each other, even if it meant he was going to be miserable. It was, he decided, a matter of asking himself if his potential happiness was worth the unhappiness of his children. "I rolled that one over and over. I couldn't stay with Maria because that was making me so unhappy, but I couldn't walk out the door because then the kids would be unhappy and I didn't want them to suffer. When you start throwing those variables together, living in the same house but as far apart as possible is the only solution you can come up with."

Paradoxically, although Allan does see the value of staying on good terms with his ex-wife and remaining close to his children, he hasn't been able to shift his feelings to more neutral ground, so he's chronically bedevilled by unresolved emotions. Maria, on the other hand, is more pragmatic. "This is the course of my life. It didn't work out. It's too bad that it didn't because we have three lovely children. It could have been great but it wasn't, and that's it. We move on." For her, it was less a matter of making an unhappy concession than of being realistic.

The decision to stay close meant that Allan and Maria had to create enough neutral space, emotionally, to allow them to cohabit. Once they'd stopped battling they could both see that, and Allan remembers that anything was an improvement over where they had been headed. "It's so much better than the kids trying to break up the fist fight between mom and dad, because that's the point we were at. Can you imagine what a pressure cooker it is when you have two people in each other's faces, each blaming the other and wanting the other to go and neither of you feeling you can go, so you are trapped, totally trapped. The only thing I can say is that we actually made it through the civil war phase into this next phase. To me, that was South Korea and North Korea, and this is the demilitarized zone."

Maria agrees that "there were fights and they got pretty feisty — not that many, but when there were, they were mean. We didn't hold back if our kids were there. If we called each other names, we did so in front of the children. We both knew that wasn't good. Not that it was really bad, but I think it could have gotten really bad if we hadn't stopped it then and there."

They had to come up with some new rules of engagement. And, as they disentangled themselves from the unhappy state of their married relationship, they had to figure out what they could be with each other. At this point neither was sure, and they made changes to their relationship incrementally. But it wasn't in Maria's nature to try to raise her daughters while maintaining the ruse of a functioning marriage, so she couldn't hide how she was feeling. "I'm not that kind of person. I've sometimes been harsh. People find me abrupt. I tell the truth the way I feel it is, and I try to be as honest with people as I am with myself, so pretending or hiding just wasn't going to do it. I had to live with this person every day, and I couldn't do it." It was painful, but practicality led them forward in their efforts to redefine how they set up the household.

❧

They took baby steps away from one way of being together toward a new way. They were groping, it was painful, and they weren't happy a lot of the time. But they kept going. "We kept talking about it to try and figure out if there was any way we could work it out," said Maria. "Shortly after that we bought this house. We knew that things were not going great, but we both wanted to stay in this neighborhood. We were both within walking distance to work, the park was close by, and the primary school was just up the street. When we moved in, we had the same bedroom and shared the same bed, but almost with a divider between us for a year or so until we decided that it was not a good idea since we were not really in love anymore or sexually active."

One of the reasons they were able to arrive at a truce was

due to the fact that they both did shift work. Allan is a journal-ist and Maria works for an airline, and both have irregular schedules. His early shift and her late shift reduced their interactions to almost nil, and Allan remembers that this gave them enough space to adjust to what was going on. "Because I was working in the morning and Maria was working in the evening, we wouldn't really see each other that much. So in a strange way, that fit where we were going in terms of our life arrangement."

They inched toward a new order of things. "We decided that Allan would have his own room and I would have mine," recalls Maria. "Eventually we just came to the agreement that for the sake of the kids we would live in the same house and try it out for a while, rather than separating physically." Repositioning themselves within the marriage was one thing, but sharing one space, and living as one household, was only going to work as a short-term solution, because being in such close quarters taxed whatever good will was left between them. They managed to do it, but barely.

⁓

Ironically, it was someone outside the family who pointed out that their escape route from each other lay within the house they already shared. One day, while Allan was confiding his frustrations to a friend, she said to him, "You guys are so stupid. You are living in the perfect house for this, don't you see?" It was true. She saw before they did that the building could easily be converted into an upstairs-downstairs duplex, making it an ideal setup for a separated couple with children. The friend suggested they take over the small apartment they rented out on their second floor and adapt the entire house to suit their needs.

Before they could undertake the stress of a renovation, Allan had to take a hard look at whether this was something he could live with. "I had to arrive at a place where I was comfortable with that decision. The comfortableness was, 'I'm not going to leave, and I'm not going to make my kids suffer. I am willing to sacrifice a lot in terms of myself and my own future happiness to make sure that happens.'" In retrospect, Maria thinks she might have had an inkling of the potential of the house right from the start. "I think in the back of my mind the idea of each of us having a floor may have been brewing when we first bought the house."

They agreed to renovate and created a unique floor plan in which each adult has an apartment with a private entrance. These two units are at the back of the building, and each has a bedroom, bathroom, kitchen and living room. Maria's is on the second floor, full of light and painted in warm pastels. Allan's is on the ground floor and looks like graduate student digs, with a hodgepodge of furniture. At the front of the house, on two floors, is a common space for the children's bedrooms. Allan and Maria each have access to this space without having to breach the other's privacy, and the children circulate freely between their parents' apartments.

Allan acknowledges, albeit grudgingly, the success of the new arrangement. For him, no other option was palatable.

"In most cases, the guy leaves, the kids stay with the mom. I couldn't do that. I think that to walk out on your family you've got to have some kind of guilt, you've got to think you deserve punishment, which is to see your kids crying at the door as you are loading your stuff into your car. I decided I wasn't going to go anywhere, no matter what happened."

ᥱᢌᵔᢒ

Staying put may have been good for the parent in Allan, but it put a real damper on his love life. Not long after he and Maria had severed their spousal ties, Allan became involved with another woman and that added to his frustration because he was caught between two worlds. He fell into a depression. "I went to see psychiatrists, psychologists. I was in a very weird space. I was living with someone I didn't want to live with anymore and having a relationship with someone who was madly in love with me that I couldn't tell anybody about. I had to carry on as if I was having a secret relationship, and I was getting no sleep because I would get up at 4 a.m. and go to work, get home around noon, have a little nap, get the kids from school, then the homework, then dinner, after dinner the dishes and putting the kids to bed, then Maria would get home from work, then I would go see my girlfriend and spend the night with her or get home at two, three o'clock in the morning, sleep an hour or two, and then get up at four to go to work again."

Allan may have been conducting a clandestine relation-ship in terms of the outside world, but as far as Maria was concerned, it was no secret. Maybe it was her practical nature, or a sign of how far she had moved away from her original emotional investment in the marriage, but it didn't rattle her. She remembers coming home some nights, before the house had been converted into two separate units, while Allan was entertaining. "He'd have her over for dinner when we were all still living downstairs. It would be late at night and they'd be out in the back, having their cigarette, sitting very close. I'd go get changed and sit there and chat, but I always felt very strange. They seemed to be perfectly at ease. It happened a few times and I was fine with it." It was not the relationship, but the implications of having another woman on the scene that presented some unexpected emotional challenges. "There was one time where . . . our tenants had moved and we had planned that we would renovate. I came home and saw her up here walking through and I thought, 'What is she doing, planning the colors?' because at one point there was some talk that she would live here also, or that she would be involved in picking up the kids after school and they would go to her house. I got territorial. It would take some adapting to have someone else doing something with my kids."

☙

Allan, meanwhile, was running himself ragged, and eventually something had to give. His outside relationship flagged; he just couldn't sustain it and hold together his life at home. He still bridles about the fact that he's living so close to the woman he doesn't want to be with anymore. In his dreams, he'd be living a different life. "What would be a perfect solution for me would be living in this house with my three kids while Maria could live wherever she wants. That's obviously not the perfect solution for my kids, so I'm willing to put up with this. Every day is a compromise."

What did annoy Maria was a legal maneuver that Allan made one summer. In Québec, mediation must precede divorce when there are children involved, and she and Allan had not yet made any moves to have their separation formally recognized. "When we got back from vacation I found this letter written to me by Allan saying that we couldn't go on like this anymore, that life seemed a charade and we should start looking into a legal separation. All along we had been discussing that we were going to do it eventually, but there was no timeline. Suddenly we had to do it."

Allan's letter provided the catalyst for Maria to make her own move toward finalizing a legal settlement. "My reaction to receiving this letter was, 'Okay, let's do it.' I quickly found a lawyer and we started three mediation sessions, and that's where we left off. We didn't finish it, and we did get into a bit of kerfuffle with Allan wanting to take the kids and move them one week on, one week off to this woman's apartment. At that point I put my foot down. 'You don't know this woman very well and you haven't been with her that long and what's the rush? The kids are going to stay in this house, Allan. You can go wherever you like and when you want to, let me know. You'll come and see the kids or you'll continue as you have been, but the kids sleep in this house, they're not moving anywhere.' That got Allan thinking a little bit more. After three sessions of mediation I don't think his relationship worked out anymore."

With the mediation stalled, the sense of urgency to finalize a legal agreement dissipated. They both acknowledge there will be financial issues to iron out, but for the moment they are in a holding pattern. Allan, a jock from way back, sees this approach to the current family arrangement in terms of a sports metaphor. "I play hockey with a guy who used to be a very good player and who just got old and slowed down. In his older years he would carry the puck very, very slowly out of his own end, almost not moving, and the other guys would be anticipating what he was going to do. He just kept moving forward and we used to call it the 'no-move move.' In a way, that's what I've done. Instead of radically and speedily going off in some direction, I've decided to slow things right down and just keep going forward and see what happens. It's a 'no-move move.'"

Allan's "take-it-slow" approach garners various responses from his friends and acquaintances, and he has noticed an interesting difference between the way men and women assess what he's doing. "To a lot of guys, I didn't have the balls to leave. A lot of women think I had the balls to stay." Allan doesn't see himself as a stalwart, by any means, and he's quite honest about that. "I don't think that I arrived at this place only because I was thinking of what is best for the kids. I'm not a hero at that level. It has a lot to do with what I can live with, and what I can live with vis-à-vis the pain I inflict on them, because there is no doubt that they are in one way or another going to get hurt in this process. I think I've done all I can do to mitigate that, so I can accept the imperfectness of this arrangement in terms of my own life."

ℯᑏᕋ

It is remarkable that Maria and Allan have been able to establish a rapport given their alienation. The peace between them may be fragile, but it has held steady, and that is an extraordinary accomplishment in itself. It's curious that two people who weren't flexible enough to make a marriage work, and who *haven't* found a friendship or even an ease between them, *have* managed to adjust to their new version of a family. It may be that their willingness to persevere with making their arrangement work is informed by their own experiences growing up, and perhaps their expectations of what constitutes family life come from what they saw in their own families, where the parents' relationships came second to the needs of the children.

Allan grew up in the Town of Mount Royal in Montréal, and his parents lived apart for long periods of time. His father was an engineer who was hired as a consultant all over the world and was based elsewhere for some years while the family stayed in Montréal. Allan remembers his father coming and going. "Sunday night the limo would come and pick him up at the house and he'd go to the airport and then the limo would bring him back Friday night. He did that for a couple of years, and throughout all that time he still coached quite a few of my hockey and baseball teams. When he was there he was totally involved, but when he was away, he was away for long stretches of time. My mom was a housewife and she ran the show. Her job was to do that, whether it was happily or not. There were long, long periods of time where she was alone."

Maria was born in a small village in Calabria, on the southern tip of Italy. "My hometown had no industry so the men left to work where the big industry was. The kids were always left with the mothers, who managed to get some kind of work. My dad went to work in the northern part of the country so he could feed his family. My idea of married couples was two parents working very hard to try and feed their kids. We were not starving, but we had only the very basics to survive. My parents were not together a lot and when they were I did not see any sort of emotional affection, or love, or anything. Not even any fights."

When her own marriage succumbed, Maria adjusted without a whole lot of anger, but while she seems accepting about overhauling her life, it's not something she has done without pain. "I have always felt quite alone doing this," she says, crying. "I don't know why I still get emotional." When she moved to Montréal she left behind family and friends, and she never managed to replace that support network. She lives far away from her own family and has always felt a distance between herself and Allan's kin. Fortunately, both families have maintained neutrality in terms of Allan and Maria's changing situation, and they continue to include Allan and Maria and their daughters in celebrating High Holidays and festivities.

❦

Allan's and Maria's journey has been one of struggling to find some kind of balance with each other, but what about their children, who are now fourteen, thirteen, and nine? This is one area where Allan and Maria have been always been in sync. From early on, they've been forthright with the children about what was going on. "Michela was six months old when we moved to this house, Amelia about five, and Olivia four," Maria remembers. "They were pretty young, but we told them from an early stage when things weren't working, especially when Allan had his own room here. We told them that we would always be there for them and that we were still going to be a family, no matter what. I don't think they understood the real meaning of it all, but we kept reminding them as the years went by that mom and dad are not like the prince and the princess anymore, we're just friends and we're here for them. As they got older they realized that we were basically separated but living in the same house. We try to keep a structured environment with the kids. I think security is really important and that was another reason we decided on this whole setup, so the kids would feel secure. Their home is still home, mom and dad are still there. They didn't have to split houses or change rooms, so nothing much has really changed in their lives. "

Whatever their individual frustrations, Maria and Allan don't believe that their unusual living arrangement has in any way harmed their three daughters. "They definitely weren't traumatized. Nobody went anywhere," says Maria. "We had heard so many horror stories of kids having to pack up each weekend and go from one house to another. A lot of these kids are our children's friends and they were not too thrilled about doing it. So far, we haven't had to, and so far it has worked. We're still living in the same house, and things haven't changed much. When I'm at work, Allan is here and he cooks; when Allan is at work and I'm here, I cook."

There *is* something that worries Maria, however. Will the girls have a damaged idea about how men and women relate to each other? Will they steer clear of ever getting married because of what they've seen happen between their parents? "They've never witnessed a true loving relationship between their mother and father. They've had it from parent to child, or child to child, but never parent to parent. We may not be traumatizing them by splitting up in the true sense of the word, but I still have these nagging questions: 'Am I skewing their view of what a real relationship is? What are they going to be like when they fall in love? How are they going to react having lived what they have lived?'"

It's hard to imagine there won't be any fallout from the time when the rancor between Allan and Maria was in full view. On the other hand, the children haven't had to endure the kind of ongoing mudslinging that governs some separations. And they know, according to Allan and Maria, that they are loved and safe and that they won't lose their home. Even if Allan hasn't been successful in moving beyond his hostility toward Maria, they have established a détente, and Maria seems to have moved comfortably into her new involvement with Allan. She doesn't need to vilify him; on the contrary, she remembers what drew her to him in the first place. "He's warm, and he was certainly very nice to me when we first met and throughout our relationship, until later. He was smart, had a good sense of humor, great taste in music, liked to hike, liked to dance, so we had things in common. Allan and I never really disliked each other; our relationship unfortunately just didn't work out. He may like me less as a person now, but I still like him as a person. There are still things that I'm really bitter about and that I don't really like, but I think Allan is a good person and he's a good father. He might even be a better father than I am a mother."

What's truly noteworthy about Allan and Maria's story is that they've managed to sustain the arrangement. Perhaps they've held on because they see the big picture, and realize just how bad it could have been between them. Maria certainly recognizes the impulse to engage in a power struggle when a marriage fails. "A lot of people are control freaks when they separate . . . they have to have the upper hand or they'll fight or make you pay. I never worried about that because I never felt Allan to be that way and I'm certainly not that way either. Although we may complain to the kids about the other half — you know, 'Dad's always making you pasta for dinner' or stupid things like that — I never was afraid that Allan would ever turn bad on me or that I would do the same on him and I don't think he talks badly to the kids about me. I may mention silly things but it's not like, 'Your dad is a creep,' or trying to turn the kids against him."

✑

The one area where real tension persists is around boundaries, which is one of the sticking points in many divorces. Allan describes their house as "open concept, with people running around everywhere. I have intense hermit tendencies so, in a way, that's probably one of the biggest gifts having children has given me," he says. "I don't have a choice, I have to open that door and there have to be people running around and when it happens, it's cool with me. I can be gregarious and I'm sociable, but really, I like the door closed, my stereo on. That's where I'm comfortable."

It's one thing for Allan to have his kids running in and out of his apartment; he can handle that. But Maria's open-door approach gets on his nerves. He feels invaded when she comes into his space uninvited. "Every time I go to look for a magazine that was on the counter over there and it isn't there anymore, it really pisses me off," he grouses. "You want it? Come to the door, come ask me for it, I'll go get it gladly and give it to you, but don't cross that line. Up until now I've avoided that confrontation and just let it percolate inside me."

It's more like the issue has been on a slow boil. Small things have become chronic irritants. For a long time, laundry was the locus of tension. "I mean, what are you supposed to do? You've got three kids, there are five people who have to do laundry," he says. The practical solution was to buy another washer and dryer for Maria's apartment so she wouldn't have to come into his place to do family laundry, but that still hasn't solved the problem of boundaries. "She still comes in here. I don't know what to do. Put a lock on the door? I want the kids to be able to come in but if I put a lock on the door and give the kids a key, it's too complicated. The only way this is going to work for me is if there is a zone only for me, and for me and the kids, and unless you see flames in here, don't come in without being invited. When I'm ready or in the mood to invite Maria in here, I'm more than happy. But I'm not a 'sharey-sharey' kind of person. 'What's yours is mine' is not me."

Allan's irritation is visible when talking about Maria's inability to understand his need for privacy. "Probably the big Italian family is part of it, but I also think that as a person Maria is much more sociable than I am and so it's natural for her. Other times I find it extremely provocative. I think she's testing me and every time she crosses that door she's waiting to see when I'm going to literally pick her up and throw her out of there. And that's where our past clashes with our present. I'm finding that pretty rough and I'm grappling with whether this is even going to work. My question is: Why is that so hard for someone else to understand? Do I have to write down that my house is mine and your house is yours on a piece of paper?"

To cope with this latest round of frustration, Allan has withdrawn into a sullen silence, which Maria has noticed but doesn't understand. "I haven't talked to Allan much, nor has he talked to me. We're not mad at each other. Work schedules haven't allowed us to run into each other, but we haven't had much to say to each other. I'm starting to think about it lately because I'm wondering, is this normal now? Is this okay? Are we really drifting that far apart? Is it going to cause problems for the kids? Should we be talking about certain things that concern the kids that we're not talking about? But Allan won't come up and he won't even come in, he'll knock and stand right by the door and talk to me. I'll be in the kitchen and he'll stand at the entry, not because he's not welcome in here, but because it's the way Allan was brought up . . . to wait until you're asked to come in, whereas I still go downstairs and borrow milk, and Allan doesn't like it, but I can't separate myself like that."

✧

There's another challenge lurking on the sidelines. Both Allan and Maria worry about how they'll fit new relationships into the home life they've created for themselves and their children. Allan feels the frustration more acutely than Maria, perhaps because he's already tried to make a liaison work and has bumped up against the parameters of his domestic arrangement with Maria. "My honest-to-God feeling right now is that we've arrived at a solution that only works because we don't have anybody else in our lives. I cannot imagine introducing another person to this relationship. Who would want to do that? I'm cornered. How am I going to get out of this? I really don't see that a woman would want to walk into a house where every time she walks in the door she can bump into her boyfriend's ex. If I met a woman who was okay with that, I would question that woman's sanity. So I've created an impossibility and that's pretty much where I'm at. It's been two and a half years since I've had a relationship and I just don't know where the hell to go with this."

Maria also feels constrained by the limits imposed by their current living situation, but she's way ahead of Allan in terms of moving on emotionally. "It wouldn't bother me if Allan does have a relationship as long as it doesn't interfere with my family and my kids in what I might view in a negative way. I have never really had a relationship, I don't think I have been emotionally ready, but I need to be loved, or have someone tell me how much they like me, love me, whatever, hug me and kiss me. I would like to think that this is not the end for me. I'm going to be fifty and I'm thinking, 'How am I ever going to meet somebody?' I'm not interested in another marriage, just something light to make me feel alive. That's the only thing I'm struggling with right now."

There are always things to struggle with when people reconfigure a marriage and a family. There are treacherous patches of black ice, and just when the journey seems under control, something will happen that can send the whole thing skidding off the road. Allan and Maria have been dealing with this reality for many years. While they both accept that the choices they've made are better for their children and for themselves as co-parents, they struggle with what it means for them as individuals. They've struck a delicate balance as ex-partners, and maybe one day they'll look back and see that it was good for them as co-habitants as well.

Maria, ever practical, has accepted the truth in the loss of any relationship, that each person has to let go of the past and get on with building a new life. If they can do it with grace, all the better. "Allan might be feeling we should have made this work somehow, since we both made this oath and commitment and brought children into it, but I've been so used to not feeling emotional, and we've been like that for so long that it feels normal. I will say it's too bad that it didn't work, but I can't do any more than that. You can't force yourself to love a person; when it's gone, it's gone. We tried."

CHAPTER SEVEN

No More Secrets

"I've learned enough to know that
what you're afraid of is always
worse than reality; it's never as bad as
you think it's going to be."
— Mary

WHEN MARC FINALLY CAME CLEAN with his wife it was like flicking a light switch. In an instant, he'd changed both of their lives. For him, it was the beginning of his liberation, but for her it was the end of a dream.

Mary thought she'd married the man she would spend the rest of her life with. They'd been together for twelve years, bought and renovated a house, and had two daughters, Madeleine and Kate. They were busy, happy, and stressed, like most parents who set themselves to the task of raising young children. But behind the appearance of a flourishing family, Marc was living a lie. He desperately wanted to be a contented husband and father, he adored his daughters and loved his wife, and yet he was restive.

Mary sensed that something was awry. Her husband had become increasingly distant and distracted, but she chalked it up to life in the family lane. "We became less and less intimate. Life goes on. It's not like you're missing something. You don't even pay attention to the fact that the passion and the romance aren't there anymore. You think, 'Well, this is what it's like when you have kids.'"

Bit by bit, the balance within the family began to falter. One night when Marc seemed particularly unsettled, Mary quizzed him about what was going on. He fled to the living room, and she followed him, demanding an answer. He remembers vividly, "I couldn't speak and I closed my eyes. I knew that the moment I told her, her life would change, my life would change, and there would be no turning back. It was like an accident, it was that dramatic. I knew the consequence of that moment: I counted to ten and I told her."

Bursting into tears, Marc confessed to his wife that he was gay. She was shell-shocked, and they both scrambled to collect themselves. For months he'd been attempting to come to grips with the secret of his sexuality, and in anticipation of a moment like this had written her a long letter trying to explain. He brought it out and they sat and read it together. Mary was stunned and struggled to digest what she was reading, and then she did something remarkable. She opened her heart to her husband. "I thought she was going to kick me out," says Marc, "but her first reaction was, 'I will always love you no matter what.' She accepted me right away."

"I think it would have been a greater challenge if I felt I had to forgive," Mary says, "but there isn't anything I have to forgive because Marc is just who he is. Should I be angry at him for telling me? No, that was the most courageous thing he could have done. If I was dealing with somebody who had done something to hurt me that would be much harder to deal with, but it was just circumstances — like bad weather."

ᶜᵞ̃ᴖ

The story of Marc's sexuality is one of ambiguity, denial, and wishful thinking. As a child growing up in a small town in Québec, he had few friends. His parents sent him off to an all-boys high school where he was always an outsider, the last kid chosen for the sports teams. "The first year I was there, I was in a dormitory and I just hated it. I cried, and I told my parents I wanted to go home." His parents had chosen the small school because they wanted him to excel academically, but looking back, Marc still feels the pain of being placed in an environment that was also meant to toughen him up. "I will always remember fighting with some boys. I was losing and one of the priests said, 'C'mon Marc, your dad sent you here so you can become a man.' My God, that was painful for me. I try not to think about it. I still have nightmares about that time. I picture myself going back there and saying, 'Listen, I am what I am!'"

Marc ignored whatever hazy sexual attraction he felt

toward men, and tried to live a straight life. "I was not sure about myself. I had a girlfriend at the age of twenty-one, the very first girlfriend I had, and I was really in love, you know? Sex was great and when we broke up it was very painful. I had convinced myself that I was not gay."

In the wake of that love affair, he did make one timid foray into the non-straight world, but it was a disaster. One day he decided to go to a gay bar and test his sexuality. "I hated it. I was nervous and I felt very uncomfortable. I had a beer and then the bartender brought me a second beer and I said, 'I didn't order that,' and he said, 'Somebody else ordered it for you.' I freaked out and left. I just left."

Throughout his twenties and early thirties he remained in denial, but he encountered friends and colleagues who sensed his true orientation. He wasn't ready to be "outed" by them and was wounded by some gossiping that went on behind his back. "Some people at the office hurt me a lot, saying to other people, 'I can't believe Marc has a girlfriend because I'm sure he's gay.' That's painful to hear, especially when you don't accept yourself."

When he was thirty-three, Marc met Mary. He had noticed her one Saturday while he was at work, and he was instantly attracted to her. "She's a very interesting woman, very outgoing, very outspoken. We started to date. Mary had so much love to give me that I thought, 'Well, I believe I can love her.'" After a year, their liaison became more serious, and they decided to buy a house together and start a family. It was a project Marc invested in wholeheartedly. "I wanted so much to love women.

Maybe fate didn't want me to come out back then because I wanted so much to have a family. I just love children."

He was also really enjoying his intimate relationship with his partner. "It was always a confirmation that I was not gay because I was able to love her. I didn't know there were different degrees, I thought it was black and white." He wondered how he could be attracted to her and be gay at the same time. "I couldn't understand that," he says.

Over the years, Marc found he was beginning to have dreams again about being intimate with men. He felt guilty and frightened as he realized that the part of him he'd been repressing wasn't going to go away. His relationship with Mary suffered. It was hard on both of them not knowing what was causing the growing rift in their love life.

"Our passion didn't come back after Kate was born," Marc recalls. "We tried to be more intimate. Mary kept telling me, 'You have to reassure me that I'm still beautiful,' which I tried to do. She said, 'You never tell me that you love me.' I could show my affection by hugging her, but I think deep down, my saying 'I love you' was like a lie to her. I didn't want to lie to her, so I avoided the topic all the time. It was like that for a few years. Mary was frustrated. I was also frustrated because I wanted to be close to her but because we were not having sex, my gay feelings were stronger and stronger. I was feeling very stressed, and my work became my refuge. Mary said, 'You are so distant from me,' and I said, 'Yes, I feel that I live in a shell now.' I was not able to love her the way that she wanted to be loved. I tried to avoid conversations or situations where I felt I was going to lie to her about myself. I would do the dishes, go back to work, go to my laptop or something. It was a difficult process and I was not talking about it to anyone."

At the same time, Marc changed jobs, moving from a hectic office environment to a start-up operation where he spent a lot of time on his own. This gave him time to reflect, and during long walks at lunch he began to ask himself some of the "what if" questions he'd never dared confront. And then one day, while he was online, he made a bold move. "I checked out bisexuality and gay fathers and suddenly I saw a profile of the 'typical gay father.' It was basically my whole history . . . it's like somebody wrote the story of my life. I thought, 'Maybe I'm not alone.'"

He needed more information and searched out a therapist who would understand his dilemma. It was the first time he had ever talked to anyone about it. He desperately wanted to find out if he was "bi" or "gay." "At that point I think I had accepted the fact that I was bisexual. I was trying to convince myself I could have a happy marriage just feeling attracted to men." He tried to rationalize his feelings by comparing himself to a man in love with his wife, but attracted to other women he had no intention of sleeping with.

Marc asked his therapist if, in his experience, people did well when they tried to make peace with their urges. "I said, 'Is it possible for me to live my marriage for the rest of my life and accept the fact that I'm bisexual and forget the whole thing?' And the therapist said, 'Do you want me to answer that question for you?' And I said, 'No.' I knew he was going to say it was not possible to ignore who you are."

✦

Over the next few months Marc wrestled with what to do. He confided in a gay friend at work, and felt huge relief about doing so. What happened in the ensuing days was a blur. "I came out to him on Wednesday and then I had to go to Edmonton on the following day and he told me he had a friend in Edmonton who's a gay father and asked if I wanted to meet him. He called his friend and I had a drink with him. It was the first time that I realized that maybe there was a positive outcome to the situation. At that point it was obvious to me that I had to come out to Mary but I didn't know when. I thought I should write a letter just in case an accident happened. It took me four hours, but I wrote a long letter on the plane [home]." That was the letter Marc gave to Mary on the night he came out to her.

Mary was deeply hurt and confused by Marc's revelation, and there were moments where she flirted with anger, but generally she held it at bay. What threw her more than the confession was how Marc's news might jeopardize their family. His decision to reconcile himself with his sexuality had jolted her to her core, but somehow she understood. "He hadn't betrayed me. He hadn't lied to me anymore than he had lied to himself. I think I felt that very early on. I just never felt angry. I kept waiting. A couple of times I felt a little bit angry because I was afraid he was prepared to throw everything away."

"There were some difficult moments," Marc remembers.

"Some days were good and some were not good. Now I could accept that I was gay and I wanted to explore that, but it was very difficult for her to accept. This is where the roller coaster started. Mary was very depressed, but my stress was gone. For years I had had this pain in my back, and then it left. The pressure just lifted."

As Mary began fumbling toward some kind of equilibrium, she did it without bitterness but not without cost. Her self-esteem plummeted. It had been shaky in the waning months of her marriage, but Marc's emergence from the shadows threw her into a state of confusion. She hadn't anticipated this emotional landmine and it had caught her quite unawares. "It made sense after he told me, but I had no idea. I felt like there was something wrong with me, which I now know is standard in mixed-orientation marriages. It's very common for the straight spouse to feel that there is something wrong with them. The gay spouse comes out of the closet, and the straight spouse goes in.

"I had to deal with feeling that I'd never had the love that I thought I'd had. That was a hard thing to deal with. But I focused on thinking, 'Well, okay, I wasn't the princess and he wasn't the prince and I guess that's the way my life was going to have to happen, but I have a wonderful human being in my life who has given me two wonderful children and I have a family.' Nobody really gets prince charming. Well maybe my mom did, but it's rare."

Mary needed some outside support and so she sought guidance from the Anglican Church. "I went to see my priest and she was amazing. She said, 'You're grieving your hopes and dreams.' I had to accept that the path I thought my life was on, and the future I thought I had, were no longer mine. She really put her finger on it. I had to rebuild a vision of the future."

Arriving at that acceptance would take enormous effort, but Mary maintained crystalline clarity about one thing: she did not want her family shattered. She did voluminous research on the subject, read every book she could get her hands on, cried a lot, and kept trying to make sense of an upside-down world. "It was all about learning to let go of the idea that I had control over what was going to happen in my life. I had to learn how to trust Marc again. I had to learn how to get hold of the facts so I could get a handle on what I knew was real and what I was just scared of. I wrote down on paper, 'This is what I know: Marc is gay and he's committed to the girls. Nothing else is certain, which means that nothing else is necessarily destroyed.'"

Marc's focus on what mattered most to him was unwavering. His wife and children were the center of his world. Ironically, he'd risked losing everything he cared about most when he came out to Mary, but it was tenderness for his wife that induced him to do so. "One of the reasons I wanted to come out to her was because I kept seeing her so sad. I could see the pain for her in our relationship and I knew I was the cause. I didn't want her to suffer and I didn't think it was fair for me to wait until I retired and then say, 'Honey, the girls are in university, I'm leaving you because I have this secret relationship with another man.' I didn't want to lie to her or to be having a secret affair."

There had been no betrayal, and that is what helped Mary to make peace with her husband's news. "I think that betrayal would have been a much harder thing to get over, although I know that people do it. I didn't have as much work to do," she says.

Still, finding a new equilibrium was not going to be easy. Mary needed to understand who her husband really was and to adjust to her new reality. "Marc and I spent a lot of time doing some family bonding, going for walks together, and spending more time together than we had. That helped to rebuild the trust so that we could build something on that, reinvent ourselves as a family, and focus on what we did have. That really gave me a lot of strength."

With the help of a therapist, Mary realized that she needed to create a bubble of time so she could find her footing. The therapist had told her to ask Marc not to do anything for six months so that she could mourn her marriage and go through the process of accepting that she was heading into a new life. Marc agreed to hold off on any decisions, and they embarked on a careful process of trying to imagine what might be possible for them. "I had to get down to what is real now. It was important to me that Marc gave that six-month commitment to give me security, so I felt that we had some solid ground to build something on."

It was one thing for Mary to hear Marc's words about wanting them to have a future together, and another to have faith that he wasn't going to take off. "I had to rebuild that trust because I knew he'd been prepared to leave if he had to. I needed to know that he wasn't going to drop another bomb on me, and I needed to feel I had complete honesty from him."

Mary was keenly aware of another reality. She'd seen how other families had fallen apart, and it wasn't something she wanted to face in hers. She was pragmatic, and even though her romantic ties to Marc had been cut, she wanted the family to remain intact. "It's like the man has the option to leave and a woman doesn't. That's sort of the default system, so I was trying to make sure this happened in a way that held him to the family because the alternative was that he might disappear. Women are never disenfranchised from their kids and their families. We're fixers in society. I think it's a female thing . . . you feel like you're the one who's the conductor, managing things. Men aren't interested in managing the emotional network of a group of people and women are."

Marc had also realized that he had to allow Mary to regain some sense of control over her circumstances. "She doesn't like to be told what to do, so I wanted to make sure she was part of the decision-making." They agreed to a go-slow deal, and focused on using the next half-year to adjust and bounce around ideas about what to do. That made sense to Mary, who is task oriented and wanted, more than anything, to work out a solution. She also recognized it was going to take some delicate footwork.

ᐣᘓᔆ

When Mary and Marc had renovated their house, he hadn't always been forthright about his own preferences. He tended to go along with her, and only later would she find out that he had wanted something else. That had been frustrating, and as they rebuilt their relationship, Mary was wary of second-guessing Marc's choices when the stakes were so high. She could see some familiar behavior patterns emerging almost immediately after he'd told her he was gay. "In that first week there was a part of me that was trying to protect him. I was torn between trying to protect myself but also trying to make things okay for him. It's that part of me that's always trying to act in a way that I know will be acceptable to him and meet his needs."

Mary recognized her tendency to be the fixer in the relationship. She also knew there was a very real threat to her own security if she wasn't able to resolve things in a way that made everyone happy. "In confrontational marriage break-ups, the guys are unhappy so they run away. It doesn't do them any good in the long run, but I didn't want to scare him, to push him away. So I had to compromise, to be patient."

A fluke event affected how things played out. Just a week before Marc made his announcement, Mary had been listening to the radio and heard me interviewed about the article I had written describing how my ex-husband and I share a duplexed house. "After that," said Mary, "there was, in the back of my mind, this option that I thought was possible, and that was important. I went out and bought the magazine and read it in secret and put it under my mattress." Knowing that we had pulled off our arrangement gave Mary confidence that she could deal with the dissolution of her marriage without every part of her life becoming unstitched. The article didn't stay hidden for long before she presented it to Marc, saying, "Why do you want to break up the family? There are options, and we need to figure out something else." The idea of sharing a house appealed to both of them and it became a metaphor for surviving as a newly configured couple.

"What was empowering was making the decision that it didn't have to be shattered, that it could be reinvented," according to Mary, who was intrigued by the possibility that she and Marc could defy convention. "You are being creative and there's a kind of 'to hell with them, I'm not going to follow their rules and be miserable, I'm going to make something of this and hold onto what is good.'"

Mary became more and more convinced that their situation was neither a disaster nor a diminishment of what they had. It was just different. "[One] afternoon I was lying on the couch in the living room and the sun was coming in. It was all very comfy and I thought, 'This is all very nice and whatever house I go to I'm still going to have this couch.' It might be a different house, but maybe because I've traveled so much I can let go of those things and know there's a difference between letting go and losing. You can let go because you know something else will come. You can let go of the house because you know you can make another space. You can let go of the specific family structure you had because you know you can build a different kind of family. It's not all or nothing. It's not 'if I lose this house I have nothing,' it's 'if I lose this house I'll have a different house. If I lose the marriage, I'll have a different relationship with Marc.'"

∞

That summer they agreed to take a vacation as a family. Little by little Mary was slowly regaining faith in their partnership. "Having those holidays together was important for re-bonding and rebuilding the family. That gave me a kind of secure space to work in, that small series of commitments. It's hard when you have the rug pulled out from under you and you don't know what you can believe anymore. Slowly, we fell right back into the same old routine." Preserving small rituals was important in that process. "He always makes me coffee every morning, because I don't know how. Planned incompetence; I can't make my own coffee. He promises me if we buy a duplex that he'll continue to make me coffee every morning."

And there were spontaneous events that gave everyone in the family pleasure. Marc remembers one day when everyone piled into the car after Mary had expressed a desire to spruce up her wardrobe. "She said, 'I think I need new clothes,' and Madeleine said, 'Yes, Mommy, you need clothes.' We decided to go shopping together — the four of us. Madeleine decided she was going to choose clothes for her mom, and Mary and I were in the change-room and Madeleine and Kate were going back and forth getting clothes. We spent at least two hours in that shop — and four hundred dollars. It was neat, you know. I could see that Mary was slowly transforming herself."

In addition to the emotional terrain they had to traverse, there were logistical issues to deal with. Sleeping arrangements had to change. Marc decided to move into an extra bedroom downstairs. By chance it was a transition that took place quite seamlessly. "I was not looking forward to the day when I said, 'Bye, Mary, I'm moving to the basement.' How do you choose that date?" Circumstance and the weather rescued him. During a heat wave, Marc headed for the cool of the basement, and he never left. "When the third night arrived Mary said, 'You just moved into the basement.' It just happened. She looked at me and said, 'Goodnight.'"

They also had to figure out how to explain the situation to their daughters. According to Marc, Kate, who is only six, has been oblivious to the import of the changes. "I never really told her that I was gay because she's too young. She knows that I am downstairs and she's never really asked why. She just accepted it. The other day she had a little friend here on a sleepover and in the morning they went to see her mom upstairs and then downstairs to see me. She said, 'This is my daddy's room,' and her friend didn't even ask why we have separate bedrooms."

Marc broke the news to nine-year-old Madeleine while the two of them were on an outing. "One day we were biking together and I think we went into a coffee shop. I decided to tell her. We are really lucky because our neighbors are a gay couple and Madeleine knows that and she understands what 'gay' means. She said, 'Wow!' Her first two questions were, 'Why are you gay?' and 'How did you become gay?' I was not expecting her to ask those questions, not right away. I told her, 'I think Daddy was born like this. Daddy really loves you.' I tried to make the whole thing positive for her. I decided to go against some of the recommendations I saw on the Internet

— to tell children this is a family secret. All the people I care about knew and I didn't want her to feel ashamed about this and think there is something wrong with it." Marc and Mary had been advised by a family therapist to be open with their children and include them, within reason, in the changes that would be occurring within the family.

On that outing, Marc had a brainstorm about how to involve Madeleine by seeking her assistance. "I said, 'I need your help to redecorate my room' and she said, 'Oh yeah, good.' And then when we were biking again, she stopped and said, 'Daddy, I'm going to have a hard time to redecorate your room. Boys like blue and girls like pink. I'm going to have to think the other way around from now on. Do you like pink, like the color of my room?' I laughed and said, 'Madeleine, Daddy will always like blue, no matter what. I don't like pink, I will never have a pink room, don't worry.' And that was it, she never asked me any more questions."

Madeleine did want to check on her mother to make sure she was all right. Mary remembers that conversation. "She was worried about me. I was honest with her and told her I was sad because I didn't have a boyfriend anymore, that Daddy was still my best friend but he wasn't my boyfriend anymore, but I'd be able to handle it. She told me that she'd help me find a boyfriend."

Mary was careful about how she set the stage in terms of any changes that were ahead, especially when she talked to Madeleine. "She has two close friends who come from separated families and in one case, her friend moves back and forth all the time between her parents. I was afraid that Madeleine would be frightened by that." Mary balked at the idea of her children becoming divorce nomads and she took pains to reassure her daughter that this would not be her fate. She explained the duplex idea to her nine-year-old, hoping she would understand that whatever changes were ahead, the four of them would be together as a family.

Marc found that his older daughter was able to distinguish between the acrimony of her friends' parents and the good will between her own when she said to him, "It's very different because you and Mommy love each other." He told her, "Yes, we still love each other and I'm not leaving the house. We may have another house together, but you will be part of the decision."

There was one family member who suffered, though. "The cat was the one that was bothered by it," said Mary. "She's very set in her ways. She tells us when to go to bed, and when to wake up in the morning, and she always slept in our bed with us. When Marc moved into the basement she was completely disconcerted. She didn't know where to sleep. For the longest time she would go up and down the stairs all night long, crying."

ご

As they began to adjust to the experience of regrouping as an unconventional family, Mary began to gain confidence that she and Marc could build something completely new. "A number of the books I read confirmed what I was coming to terms with, that there was no benefit in being angry or in tearing your life apart if you don't have to." But it really irked her that the preponderance of materials she picked up about divorce were so bleak. "They all assumed that you go off and have separate lives and have nothing to do with each other. Some of them said you shouldn't have holidays together, you shouldn't be talking to each other, because you have to get on and start your new life. I have a friend who is separated and when her daughter is with her ex, she doesn't phone her, she doesn't talk to her, because her psychologist said that in the first year it is much better if the child has complete division of their lives. To me, that's just so completely false."

As she searched for alternatives to the traditional divorce model, Mary kept coming upon stories of disaster. "Everybody says that kids are resilient, they'll survive. But that doesn't mean that split houses are the best thing for them and that we can't find something even better." The assumption that it was the kids who should have to move back and forth between two parental homes and live out of a suitcase riled Mary. This was not what she wanted for her daughters. "I am really curious how many positive alternatives exist that nobody ever talks about. Only angry people seem to talk. If you were living in a terribly confrontational and disruptive, dysfunctional situation there might be value in that, but I'm not. We're still a family."

They decided to spend their three-week vacation in Victoria with Mary's family. "We knew we had to tell her parents," said Marc. "They were celebrating their sixtieth wedding

anniversary and we didn't want to tell them that news beforehand and break up the party. Mary and I were so nervous.
I'd been able to find a lot of resources on the Internet, but I
can tell you there is nothing about how to come out to your
father-in-law. Mary joked about it, saying, 'It's your news,
you tell them. It's your punishment.'"

Mary's father is a little deaf, so what ensued had moments
that, in retrospect, amuse both Mary and Marc. "It was almost
a comedy. We had everything planned. We were going to tell
them on Monday night so they'd have two days to think about
it before we left. We put the girls to bed about 9:30 in the
evening, and we were sitting, the four of us, in the living room.
Then her father fell asleep. I didn't know what to do. Mary
looked at me and gave me the high sign: not tonight. 'Oh shit!'
I thought. The whole day was stressful for nothing."

The next night they knew they had to do it. "My heart was
pounding, and Mary said, 'Dad, Mom we have something to
tell you. Marc will tell you the news.' I started to say, 'Mr. Allen,
I've struggled a bit with my life,' but he couldn't quite hear
me and said, 'What did you say?' I looked at Mary for help, so
Mary said, 'Marc is struggling with his life.'

"Mary was holding my hand the whole time, and telling
them that we want a functional family. We told them about the
duplex idea to reassure them that the girls are in good hands.
After a long pause, Mr. Allen said, 'On behalf of both of us, we
accept you.' That was very moving."

Marc remembers that Mary's mother worried about her
daughter and asked later, "Can you just live like this for the

rest of your life?" Mary told her that eventually she and Marc would likely separate because he needed to explore and live his life. When they heard the news, other family members called to say they still considered Marc part of the family. Mary's parents invited the whole family to go to Hawaii with them the following summer, and Marc says, "I wasn't sure if I was going to be invited because of the situation, but they insisted." In the end, five families — fourteen people — took that trip and had a wonderful time.

The next hurdle was telling Marc's own family. Stoked by the positive reaction they'd received from unveiling their secret to Mary's clan, they headed to Québec City. Marc confided in his younger sister first. He was alone with her when she asked, "So, how are things going at home?"

"I said, 'Fine . . . there are some difficult moments,' and she said, 'What's wrong? Are you sick?' No. 'Do you have a girlfriend?' No. 'A boyfriend?' I started to laugh. No, but . . . ." Once he told her the situation, she was very supportive.

Marc had worried about telling his parents. He was concerned about his father's failing health, so he decided to tell his mother first. "My mom is cool as a cucumber. I've only seen her crying three times in her life and each time was at a funeral. Her family, which is a big family of fifteen, doesn't show emotions. Her reaction was, 'Well, you're forty years old and you know what you are doing. If you are happy, so be it.'" Even now Marc says he has no idea how she really felt.

"After I told my mother, I told my father. He started to cry. But he wasn't crying because of me being gay, it was his fear that he'd lose access to his grandchildren. And he asked me, 'Am I going to be able to see Mary?' I said, 'Of course. She is part of your family just like I am to [her family]. At that point Madeleine arrived and it was the four of us together. I said, 'Madeleine, I just told Grandma and Grandpa about our news.' The fact that Madeleine knew helped them to accept this, and the weekend after I told them, my father called me and said, 'You are always going to be our boy.'

"They came to see us a few weeks ago. We needed to redecorate Mary's bedroom as it's a new beginning for her, and I had asked my father to help me. It was the first time they had come to see us in our new family situation, and they saw my bedroom downstairs. So my father helped me to paint Mary's room. It was for her, not for me, and it was a way for him to show us that he accepted the situation."

❧

Mary believes that she and Marc will remain kin to each other for the rest of their lives. It's a link she wants to preserve and nurture. "I think the bottom line to me is that when you have kids, the words 'till death do us part' gains a kind of biological imperative. It's up to us if we are going to be functional or dysfunctional. Marc and I are still best friends. We like each other, and you don't throw away love, you don't undo it. If it's there, you nurture it. The problem is there's no model for doing that when your marriage ceases to exist. You have to invent it."

Along the way, Mary and Marc have been surprised and

stung by some of the negative reactions to their efforts from people outside the cocoon of their families. "Nobody out there seems to understand," Mary says, recalling some of the thoughtless comments she'd heard, like 'How can you talk to each other?' 'How can you put up with each other?' 'Why aren't you angry? 'You must be in denial,' 'You must be repressing something,' or 'You must be victimizing yourself.' "No," she says emphatically. "I'm trying to take control and hold my family together. As far as I'm concerned my marriage is an annulled marriage. It may be null and void, but my family is still a viable family."

At this point she is a bit weary of trying to help the world make sense of their unorthodox approach to the circumstances. "I don't want to tell anybody now, because it's so complicated. I don't want to explain myself. The last person that we told phoned me later and said, 'I don't think you should go for a duplex.' When I asked why not, she said, 'You'll be really hurt if Marc brings home boyfriends.' She was underestimating both of us. She thought that he was going to turn into somebody else and put his family aside and only think below the belt. He's not going to bring home boyfriends until he's serious about them and if he's serious about them he'll bring them home to get us to check them out.

"I was angry because she thought that I would be prepared to destroy my family because I might feel some pain. If he meets somebody else, it's going to hurt no matter where he lives. I'm quite prepared to deal with what comes, but I'm not prepared to lose my children for fifty percent of their lives."

Some of Mary's strength has come from her faith, which infuses her entire philosophy of life. "I'm Christian so I've always had this belief that God can't give me everything I want, but maybe God can give me the strength to handle what comes at me and get over it. People are amazingly resilient and I think every human being has the capacity to build their life. People allow themselves to destroy their lives but I think everybody has the capacity to get over that hump if they can find the strength. The only thing I'm afraid of now is not knowing what situation we're going to get into. I guess I have fear about how I'll feel if Marc finds a new partner, but that's something to deal with then. You know, I think I've learned enough to know that what you're afraid of is always worse than reality; it's never as bad as you think it's going to be. I have faith that whatever happens I can handle it."

But what about her future and any possible partners who might come into her life? What if she met somebody who couldn't deal with the fact that Marc lived in the house? "I figure if I met somebody, I'd have to get them to meet Marc before I really started going out with them. If they have a relationship with him beforehand then he's not really 'the other.' I'd want to make the family situation upfront from the beginning so that there are no surprises."

༄

Both Marc and Mary did begin new relationships — at around the same time. Marc describes the early stages this way. "It was a little odd at the beginning, or 'weird' as Madeleine said, but everyone got used to each other's new friends. The neighbors all know about our situation and, I am sure, have been talking a lot about all the ins and outs from our place."

On Mother's day, Marc invited the whole gang to celebrate. He reserved a table for eight at a restaurant and Mary invited her new entourage along. "[Her new beau] has two girls, a little older than Madeleine . . . actually, one of them was, and still is, our babysitter. It was fun and this extended family event made everyone more at ease with each other," Marc says. Marc and Mary are taking a "more the merrier" approach to their expanding new family. It's working for the kids, too, according to Marc. "They both have lots of opportunities to know my friend and Mary's friend and everyone is accepting each other very well. Madeleine is amused about having so many men around her now."

"Once you have kids, you're family for better or worse," Mary observes. "That's just the way it's going to be. You're family until death do you part. You can have good relations or bad. Estranging somebody and trying to pretend you can have a life without them just makes it more difficult when you do have to deal with them. Just because Anglo North American society has come up with a model that says you have to be a nuclear family doesn't mean that extended families don't exist all over the world."

In an effort to affirm their viability as a family and define their relationship according to their own values, Mary and Marc chose to observe the first wedding anniversary after their split in a special way. Getting married had been an important statement to one another and the world. They didn't want the anniversary date to become a mark of failure, a symbol of what hadn't worked. They thought carefully about it and decided to celebrate by privately recommitting themselves to each other. They went to lunch at their favorite restaurant, a converted old house in the country. Marc remembers, "We decided to just focus on each other. If we can't commit as husband and wife, we can recommit as friends." They repeated the vows they'd made to each other nine years before, and then made another gesture to symbolize their ongoing relationship. Each removed the wedding band from the left hand and placed it on the ring finger of the right hand. Together, they had come out to the world.

CHAPTER EIGHT

Crossing the Rubicon

Once the words came out of my mouth,
there was no going back."
— LJ

WHEN LJ ENDED HER RELATIONSHIP with Peter, it was swift and final. "One day we had this big fight. I don't even know what it was about, and he said, 'You know this is never going to work,' which is something I had heard just about every week that we were together. I said, 'You're right, it isn't.'" Once she'd said the words, that was it.

It was a drastic move. They had two small children, a seven-year-old and a six-month-old baby LJ was still nursing. She was just beginning to get on her feet financially after graduating from acting school, but she'd had it with years of disharmony and conflict. That squabble pushed her over the line. "I think he was shocked. That was the first time I had

ever really said, 'I can't do this.' Then I couldn't go back . . . I
needed to be free of our relationship."

LJ was resolute. The thought of going solo allowed her
to imagine a happy life for the first time in years. "I felt this
remarkable sense of freedom because I had spent all those
years trying to make it work, trying to bash this square peg into
a round hole and going at it from every side . . . really earnestly
doing what I thought was best. But we were just never ever
meant to be together. We wanted such different things from
life. I couldn't have the life I wanted with him. I just couldn't.
He was a wonderful dad but a terrible partner to me."

Peter and LJ had met when they were both twenty-seven
and working in a posh downtown restaurant. She was an
aspiring actor, he was an underemployed musician and theirs
was a classic case of opposites attracting. LJ was easygoing
and athletic, with tight blonde curls and a radiant smile. Peter
was the funny guy at a party, but in private tended to be dour
and dark.

Eight months into their romance, LJ discovered she was
pregnant — a "cervical cap" baby, she ruefully remembers.
Peter wanted nothing to do with having a child. "I was madly in
love with him, which was insane," she says, "because he didn't
want to be in any kind of a committed relationship. Ultimately
it was my choice. He really didn't want me to have the baby,
even if he wasn't going to be with me, because he didn't want
to know that he had a baby out there in the world."

LJ considered terminating the pregnancy, but changed
her mind. "I phoned Peter and told him and then we spent

the next eight months negotiating whether or not he would be a part of it." Negotiations included a trip to a Caribbean island where friends had convinced them they could make good money working. "I thought I'd have all this money for the baby, and we wanted to find out whether or not we could actually live together, so I took him down there," LJ says. "Paid for the whole trip."

They'd only been there a month when her father was diagnosed with a brain tumor. LJ had never really had a relationship with her father, but his health was precarious and she felt uncomfortable being so far from home, so she returned to Toronto. Peter went back to Montréal.

Peter moved in with his parents and stewed about what to do. He remembers this period as being an emotionally charged time. "I was quite depressed," he admits. "I was pretty mixed up as to what I wanted to do and it just felt like this was a huge decision to make." After a few weeks he'd made his decision. He did *not* want to be involved in having the baby.

LJ cobbled together some work while she tried to plan a future as a single mother. Then, in an instant, everything changed. During a visit LJ made to her family, her little niece died suddenly and LJ, three months pregnant, was devastated. She telephoned Peter and asked him to come and he did. After seeing the family's grief over their loss, he decided to try on his "father hat." They went back to Toronto and moved in together.

The shock of that death had prompted them to see what they could make of their relationship, but Peter was always ambivalent about it, and it showed. "He didn't tell his parents I was pregnant until about three weeks before our daughter was born," says LJ. Meanwhile, each of Peter's three brothers would phone her several times a day just to see how she was and to find out if their parents knew yet.

Peter remembers the pregnancy as a difficult time. "We were going to have a baby and neither one of us had jobs or money. It was tough — and continues to be — so I went back to a restaurant that I had been working in and ended up staying there for four years."

❦

When Taylor arrived she was colicky and clung to LJ. For the first three months, she screamed from six in the evening until three in the morning. "The first time she slept during the day," says LJ, "I phoned my sister to see if I should take her to the hospital and my sister asked why. I said, 'She's sleeping!' and my sister said, 'She's a *baby*. She's supposed to sleep.' The screaming was hard and I think that Peter was afraid of her, so he kept leaving everything up to me. And I kept taking that power that mothers have with their babies. I never left her."

The anxiety also played itself out in a dance about money. Peter hadn't followed his heart, and he found it hard to let LJ focus on acting and follow hers. "Our life together was always strained," she says. "There was this sense that I really had to bring in a lot of money or he was going to leave. So here I was with this tiny baby, trying to make enough money so that everything would be split evenly."

LJ is still bitter about Peter's lack of interest in her acting, which to her was tremendously important. "I would write a play, produce it, and put it on, but Peter wasn't supportive of my artistic endeavors. I would come from a rehearsal and people's husbands would come to pick them up, and they knew everything because they would be rehearsing lines with their partners. Peter didn't know anything about [what] I wrote. He didn't want to know, didn't want it to interfere, didn't want to put any kind of a burden on himself."

In Peter's view, LJ was always rushing around, which unsettled him. "We're quite different people. My work is very social and my private life is very private. I don't have as much of a desire to be busy all the time. Some people like to live in this constant state of 'I've got so much going on, yet I'm taking on more,' and I just don't like that. I have one good friend I've known from when I was a kid, I have my kids, and a couple of guys I work with. But I spend a lot of my time by myself. . . just kind of do my own stuff. I don't make a lot of big social plans."

❧

The space between them widened. They led parallel lives, he working double shifts at the restaurant and she struggling to balance working and motherhood. They patched together an arrangement that they could sustain — one of them was always on baby duty while the other worked. Although both were devoted to their young daughter, their relationship remained shaky and they were always on the verge of separating.

LJ wrestled with conflicting feelings. On one hand, she was exasperated with Peter, but on the other, she kept trying to fix the relationship. "It's that fairy tale. . . that I'm going to magically make him want the same things I want. Over time I knew that wasn't going to happen and I did start having a life of my own."

LJ understood that Peter required a lot of freedom and time alone, but she didn't want to limit her life or Taylor's. "When Taylor was about six, she started to notice that every-one else's daddy was [around] but hers. I think that probably contributed to my being able to leave. It didn't make sense to have all the stress of trying to keep the family together."

The lack of connection seeped into every part of LJ's life, creeping into her awareness while doing even the most mundane things. "I can remember being in the supermarket on Friday nights when we were still together, and feeling the most incredible loneliness. I would see these couples shopping together and I would just think, 'How is this possible that I've made such a mess?'"

In spite of her discontent, LJ became pregnant again, this time on purpose. She explains the curious decision to have another child with a man she wasn't happy with. She didn't want Taylor, then seven, to grow up by herself, and Peter agreed that it would be good for Taylor to have a sibling. When Sarah was born, Peter and LJ had a couple of months that were quite euphoric. Then the old problems resurfaced and it was clear that they were just not on the same path in life. Paradoxically, Sarah's arrival liberated LJ enough to consider building a new life without Peter. As she became less and less able to accept the constant friction between them, she had to confront some uncomfortable questions about herself. "My relationship with Peter was a complete repetition of my relationship with my parents. My father was absent, and now I was with an absent partner who was very critical of me . . . the way my mother was. I had found my mother and my father all in one person. Oh, my God!"

❧

LJ's mother had been raised as a Catholic, but for mysterious reasons had told everyone that she was Jewish, a myth that she maintained for the rest of her life. "She created stories for herself to make people think certain things of her," LJ said. "She came from a working-class background and my father was very wealthy, and the big joke was that my father's parents were anti-Semitic and would not quite accept my mother."

LJ's parents separated when she and her sister were young, then reunited and later had a son. "For the two years that they were separated, I don't think I saw my dad. He was just a classic absentee father." Her grandfather was a pedophile, she says, "but my mother would never admit that he had done anything wrong, even when she learned years later of what he had done with my sister and me."

LJ's experience with family deception and familial warfare informed a lot of the effort she put into rebuilding her own family. When she finally looked hard at the truth of her relationship with Peter instead of the façade, she was forced to acknowledge that, like her mother, she too was living a lie. She knew from experience how poisonous it could be when children are forced to choose sides in an acrimonious separation, and there was no way she was going to take her daughters down that path. "It was really important that when we did split up, we do it right. I didn't want the kids to ever feel like they had any responsibility or that their loyalties were divided, although they do still struggle with that."

Peter had not grown up with a positive family model either. The second-oldest of four boys, his childhood had its own allotment of smoke and mirrors. "My dad was a doctor; my mom was a nurse. They were distinctly separate their whole lives. They were doing that typical family thing of that generation. You go to high school, meet, get married, the woman gives up her career, the husband does the supporting, and the woman raises the kids. They really stuck to that as long as they could, but there was a lot of animosity between them.

"My dad cheated on my mom early on and has a daughter somewhere out there that we've never spoken about. I just found that out within the last few years. That created a big rift with my parents."

Peter's father was an alcoholic and suffered from "a bit of social anxiety," according to Peter. "He was semi-retired all his life. He never really made enough money. He was terrible with money, and subsequently we are all terrible with money. My parents did not teach us any coping mechanism because they didn't know it themselves. It was always panic. Just a letter from the government and, 'Oh my God, we're going to be broke and poor!' That was my mom's biggest fear, to be on the street and be poor."

⁓

There are two ways to respond to bad situations — either shrink from the world or leap out toward it. Be weak or be strong. LJ took the direct approach. Peter, on the other hand, was inclined to let things drift. For him, the relationship died with more of a whimper than a bang.

Their agreement to separate allowed both LJ and Peter to relax. By ending a bankrupt romantic relationship, they were able to remodel the parenting relationship that still had some currency. Nevertheless, it was brutally tough to break it to a seven-year-old who would be devastated by the news. "It was the worst day of my life," LJ recalls. "We just sat her down, said that we had something to talk to her about and that she knew Mommy and Daddy weren't always very happy together and that we liked life quite differently from one another and that we had decided that it would be better for all of us if we lived apart, and that it wasn't anything to do with her. She was hysterical for several hours. She just wanted it to go away, she wanted it to not be true. She begged, she pleaded, she accused us of everything. Sarah doesn't have nearly the scars that Taylor has because Sarah didn't live with us together for long. She didn't live in the tension, ever."

LJ remembers with some fondness the time between when they decided to separate and when Peter actually moved out. "Those were probably our best months, of all the years we spent together. There were a couple of really bad angry fights, some really unpleasant moments in that time, but we were starting to actually have a conversation which wasn't just defensiveness, or blaming, or me trying to get him to live my life and him trying to get me to leave him alone." Peter was relieved that the split had come. "It was the relief of not coming home to a tense house, always having somebody sort of in a snit at you, and I'm sure she felt relief in the same way."

But figuring out where Peter would go took some time. Both wanted to live close to each other for the sake of the girls. They stayed in the same house for six months, negotiating how they were going to do everything and where he was going to live. Then Peter moved into temporary basement digs in the house of a friend of LJ's, "an apartment which I thought I'd be in for two months, but where I stayed for six years." LJ helped him get his place set up and do his first grocery shopping. She even went to his apartment sometimes and made Taylor's breakfast before he went to work.

❧

As soon as LJ was on her own, she made a beeline for what she really loved doing professionally, an act of independence that brought her great satisfaction. "The minute we separated, I got an agent, got a waitressing job and started acting again. We were all having so much fun, and I was taking classes again and doing what I wanted to do and making it work." On the homefront, the mood of the house changed palpably. "I was a totally different person. We had joy in our house for the first time. We'd put music on after dinner and dance. The house was full all the time, it was always entertaining. I was really catching up after years of not being able to do that." Taylor remembers this as a happy time too. "I was eight or nine, so I went through my make-up phase then and it was really fun being with my mom and my sister. We could all sit around and watch movies and paint each other's nails and stuff."

LJ had always known that it would be a financial challenge to go it alone, but as an artist she had eked out a modest living all her adult life. She and Peter settled on sharing the children's costs, but she didn't ask him for support, even if the girls were with her more of the time. She admits this was partly for her own selfish reasons. "I'd always done more than he'd done and I didn't ask for support because I knew he would have demanded to have the girls more. I was happy to have them, so I was happy to pay more. I know that's a terribly manipulative thing to admit, but it's the truth."

They devised an arrangement whereby Peter would have the girls for a couple of nights a week. They lived separately, but maintained many of the family traditions that would have mattered to the children. Birthdays and holidays were always celebrated together. LJ worked weekends as a waitress so she could be at home with the children during the week and Peter could have the girls on the weekends. She weaned Sarah quickly to make it easier for Peter to take her. LJ never liked being away from her daughters for even a day, but she wanted to ensure that the girls would continue to have contact with their father.

There were times when Taylor expressed frustration with the arrangement. "She would often complain, when she was home with me, that she hated having two houses. She wished that her parents could just be together, but I think she quickly realized that life was a whole lot better. I remember having conversations with her about it and her saying at quite a young age, 'You and Daddy don't fight the way so-and-so's parents do. You and Daddy are friends still.' And in fact, we were friends in a way we really hadn't been for a very long time. I think it was better for everyone."

Neither LJ nor Peter indulged in fault-finding or attempts to create a villain. Even Peter, who had been "left" by LJ, did not play the blame game. "I think we found peace, somehow," says Peter. "We were never holding tons of animosity—at least I wasn't. It's not really giving up, it's just that you have to put in focus what your relationship with this person is. It's a new dynamic. I don't go to LJ for personal support. I know she'd be there in a second if anything really serious happened, but that part of our relationship is gone." This absence of malice facilitated the rebuilding. They kept their understanding flexible and spelled each other off when necessary. Their work lives were often in flux, and when one or the other had to change a shift, the other accommodated. Taylor remembers the elasticity of the schedule. "We never had a week on, week off schedule, because I think they were still friends so they could talk about it, where I think some people whose parents just hate each other can't, their schedule's really rigid. There was routine, but if they needed to switch, they could switch."

꙳

Then a new person entered LJ's life. She was working in a gay bar where Jon was the chef. "We were the token straight people," she says, laughing. "Jon's the last person I would ever have imagined ending up with. He was the kind of guy that I ran away from all my life — the guy who was too nice, or there weren't enough sparks, or there wasn't enough this, or there wasn't enough that, or you could convince yourself after one date that they were too goofy."

But LJ was older and wiser now and had given some serious thought to her romantic choices of the past. She was determined to break her unhealthy patterns and began to date Jon. The relationship took off like a rocket. "It was fast, very fast. He and I want all the same things out of life. He's never going to be wealthy, he's not interested in money, but he's such a decent human being, so conscientious and with an amazing generosity of spirit."

Jon was born in southern Israel on a kibbutz organized around the utopian principle that individuals in the community own nothing and share everything. "The way it was when I grew up, everything belongs to everybody," he explained. "So even if you got a package from someone, you shared it with everyone. It was like a commune and people had high ideals."

Jon lived there until he was sixteen. "When I was born, the way it worked is that you spend a few weeks with your parents but then you go to a nursery with a few other babies and their caregivers. You grow up with the same group, more or less the same age, and both parents can go to work. When your parents come back from work, they take you home, spend time with you, then take you back to the nursery where you sleep."

Jon fell hard for LJ and they were a good match. Unlike Peter, Jon was not unsettled by LJ's noisy social world. He had grown up with eighteen other kids as well as his nuclear family. Wary about forcing the girls into the position she'd been put into herself as a child, LJ took her time before introducing them to her new love. "My mother pushed her boyfriends on us," said LJ. "She would be dating someone for a week and suddenly we were expected to behave as if they were the be-all and end-all and that we had this close relationship. It was just all such nonsense. I didn't ever want Taylor to feel she had to do that or that she had to be disloyal to her dad."

When LJ and Jon became serious, LJ felt it was time everyone met. She had started seeing Jon in December but didn't introduce him to the girls until June, at the end of the school year. Taylor was ten and Sarah was three. "It was pretty much a disaster from the beginning," she admits. "It was fine with Sarah because she was a toddler, but it was hard with Taylor, who resented and resisted him and wasn't interested in any way."

A year after they'd met, Jon and LJ decided to get married, and he moved in about five months before the wedding. Taylor gave Jon a hard time. LJ understood her daughter's feelings but insisted on détente within the household. "I said, you

don't have to like this guy; you don't have to have a relationship with him. He's not your choice, he's my choice. You do
have to be respectful, and you do have to understand that he
is living in this house and he's an adult in this house so he
has certain rights because of that, but it's all negotiable, and
I don't expect you to have any relationship with him, if you
don't want to."

The standoff between Jon and Taylor did not extend to
Peter. The two men got along famously right from the beginning. Peter remembers his early reaction. "When LJ first met
Jon, it kind of came out of nowhere and very quickly they were
living together and married. There was an adjustment period
for me for sure, but I was lucky, I had a great girlfriend then
too, so it softened the blow. In the end, I felt better because
when we separated, if I heard a siren I was always thinking,
'Something's wrong, oh my God.' Having Jon there, I felt more
comfortable. And once I met him I liked him right away. He's
a very nice guy."

Jon had a similar reaction to Peter. Neither seemed to feel
the need to stake out territory with the other, and Jon is quite
sanguine about his feelings about LJ's ex. "I'm not jealous,
in general, not at all. I know that she's committed to me and
I'm committed to her. And I knew that the kids had a dad and
I'm a stepdad. I knew that LJ was in no way wanting to be with
him, so it's not something I even worried about. If we hang
out together, we have a great time."

෴

The new family found its own kind of balance, and Jon, whose experience of family life was so much different than that of LJ or Peter, brought his own perspective to the situation. "If you divorce in an agreeable way, especially in an arrangement where it is peaceful and people are satisfied with their lives, you show kids on a deeper level that life can be good and you can make it good."

All successful families transform over time, adapting to the changing needs of each member of the clan. This reconfigured little unit – LJ and Peter and the girls, and now Jon – chugged along for a few years, with relative peace and calm. For years, Peter had been less than two minutes' walk from LJ and the children. Then the house where he was living was sold. At the same time, LJ and Jon had been considering whether to buy a house in another part of town, or stay put and keep renting. They opted to remain in the house and neighborhood they loved, and a far-fetched idea crept onto the radar screen.

It began with a joke. While Peter was apartment hunting, LJ and Jon were calculating how to lighten their monthly costs, and Jon said facetiously to LJ, "We need another tenant to supplement our income. Let's get Peter. It's fine with me, because I get along with him. It would be good for the kids, especially for Sarah because she's really attached to him."

The idea grew incrementally. LJ approached Peter and said, "You know, if you don't find a place, you could always stay with us for a month or two." Which is exactly what happened. Peter moved in, ostensibly for a month. It was an easygoing negotiation, as Peter remembers it. "We've tried very hard to make it so it wouldn't get to a point where, like an awful divorce, you can't be in the same room with each other. Neither one of us wanted that. We bounced it off the girls and Sarah especially was happy. Taylor said, 'Yeah, that would be fun.'"

The house they were all going to live in is by no means palatial. It's a modest two-story, detached house on a tree-lined street in the downtown core. A roomy kitchen with a big table serves as the focus of family life and looks out onto the postage-stamp back garden. There's a small living room at the front of the house, and Sarah's and Taylor's rooms are on the second floor. LJ remembers how they decided who would go where. "We have a room and a kitchen upstairs that [Jon and I] were using as a bedroom and an office. We moved out of that space and gave it to Peter so he's got more privacy, and we moved down into a room beside the kitchen."

Peter was excited about finding the right kind of space for his needs, which are simple. "I would be out there spending fifteen hundred bucks a month on rent. It just made sense to go in there at six hundred bucks and be with my kids — and have them see that it's all pretty fine, pretty good. It's an easier transition for the kids, there's not two of everything, that really day-to-day stuff."

What works for the adults doesn't always fit perfectly for the children in these situations. Taylor, who was a teenager, had a mixed response to the whole thing, but felt unable to articulate her true feelings. To her, the new escapade her parents and Jon were about to embark upon was already a fait accompli. "They mentioned, 'Oh yeah, is that okay?' and I had to say yes. If I had said no, they would have done it anyway. It's bizarre. And if my dad picks up the phone or something, it's weird telling my friends when they ask, 'Aren't you at your mom's house?' and I say, 'Yeah it's the same house.' I'm not annoyed by it. If it had happened when I was nine or something, it would be different. My sister loves it. She's totally thrilled by it, because she doesn't really remember having my parents in the same house, whereas I remember them splitting up and what it was like. So now it's like, 'What are you *doing*?'"

Taylor's memories of when her parents were living together, not all of them pleasant, made her cautious about getting too excited about having her father move in, but LJ remembers the pure joy her younger daughter experienced knowing her father was living under the same roof. "For Sarah particularly, it's really nice to see her dad every day. The first few weeks were just heartbreaking, she was so ecstatic. She would literally kick open the door and say, 'Mom! Dad!' It was this little body's pleasure in being able to say both of those words in the same house; it was overwhelming for her."

⟳

Blending families is always a complicated business, and it rarely happens without some stress. This unusual configuration posed unique challenges, especially for the girls. Taylor's ambivalence was apparent from the start, but Sarah's unmitigated delight gave way to some confused feelings about having both men in the same place, and the pleasure of having her father living there clouded her relationship with Jon. As LJ remembers, "Sarah was so little, they bonded quite quickly, but once Peter moved in, Sarah started to feel, 'Uh-oh, if I like Jon, that means I don't like my dad.' That's been her struggle the last little while. I think she's starting to understand that it's okay, she's allowed to like both of them and only one of them is her dad."

Peter's role as a parent to the girls had been somewhat circumscribed from the outset, but what surprised LJ was that once he was back in the same house as his children, he spent less time, not more, with the kids. "The first few months were hard for them because they came face to face with how little he does for them," LJ said. She remembers that things went from rosy to wretched for Sarah. "It was really good for her for the first little while. And then it was really hard for her, because she had these divided loyalties and she realized that her dad doesn't do a whole lot. So we had to talk about Daddy and his limitations."

Jon had grown up in an environment where work was something shouldered equally by everyone in the community, and he had always fully shared the running of the house with LJ. Peter, on the other hand, tended to hole up in his room when he joined the household and only took responsibility for the children on Thursday nights. The contrast between Jon's involvement in the girls' lives and Peter's became really obvious. As LJ describes it, "Jon rarely says no. He takes the initiative when he can clearly see what needs to be done, practical things, laundry, that stuff, and I never have to tell him what needs to be done, he just does it. I think because he grew up in a kibbutz where there's no such thing as male work or female work, it's all just work that needs to be done."

That highlighted an imbalance that had always been present but was not always obvious to the children when there were separate houses. "Taylor had a really huge burst of anger. For a long time she resented Jon for being so good and she just hated that he was. She wanted him to be awful. How dare he be better than her dad at supporting stuff that she does and being there for her mom and all these things? It was very hard for her. She's come through that I think now."

LJ had to respond to Sarah's questions and anger. "She's a very intuitive kid. She'd ask, 'Mommy, how come my daddy is lazy? How come Jonny works so hard?' And then she'd get mad because she wanted her dad to be doing those things for her. And somehow it was my fault. . . I was somehow making this happen. We had to do a lot of talking about that. We had to identify that they both had strengths and weaknesses and what they were. I think she's starting to come around. She was starting the 'You're not my dad' thing for a while, and she hasn't really been doing that lately. Jon and Peter back each other up with the kids, so the lines are clear. She doesn't have to negotiate them."

What wasn't obvious was that sometimes Peter would stay out of sight in the house because he didn't want to interfere or undermine Jon's role. "I've had to adjust too, coming into their home," Peter explains, "and I try to make myself pretty scarce sometimes. I know I'm allowed to be downstairs with them and stuff like that, but I know if I'm downstairs, Sarah will probably come to me, and I like her to go to Jon because he's a good guy and they have a great relationship."

LJ still wishes Peter could figure out how to play a larger role in their daughters' lives. "It's not that they're not close, they're very close, it's just that he's not very involved. So if I don't say so-and-so has a concert and I don't buy the ticket, he doesn't go. I kind of have to set it up and inform him and tell him everything that's happening. I don't know about Sarah so much, but Taylor's got a few friends whose dads are pretty amazing and very involved in their lives and I know she feels a certain amount of resentment about that. But she also really understands him."

❧

The house has, in its first year, carried on much the way it did before Peter's arrival, according to Jon. "Basically we run the house. He's like renting the place. So that's the dynamic. He only has to take care of his place, so we take care of cleaning and the dinners, and everything. On his night when he has the kids, he feeds them and makes sure that Sarah does her homework. Peter takes Sarah to school in the mornings. He uses the washing machine and we share the washroom. Now he works nights, so if he wants to do laundry, he can do it during the day and there isn't a lot of interaction. If there's a family event or parties, he's always invited. As far as decisions about what to do with the kids or issues of discipline, if it's something that LJ and I can work out together then he lets us decide," Jon says. "If there's something more serious, then we sit together and decide on what to do and how. And in general, we talk about things if there's something we don't agree about."

One of the unexpected benefits of having two male figures in a household is that they each have things to share with the kids. LJ values this. "A lot of the modeling and stuff that you would hope they could get from their father, they really get from Jon. Taylor has chosen a boyfriend who is very similar to Jon — very quiet and incredibly thoughtful. He's just lovely to be around. He's also a musician, and they seem to have a lovely quiet time together. And I find when Taylor's boyfriend is here, Peter will come out a little more. I don't think he knows how to relate to a teenage daughter, but he can relate to her boyfriend so he'll come out. That's the only time I've ever seen Peter play with Taylor; he'll play guitar and Taylor will get on her violin and they'll all play together and it's kind of nice."

LJ also recognizes that there's only so much she can ask of Peter. "I think there's a lot of tolerance, and in some ways there's a lot of taking the path of least resistance. I don't push for things I think would be better because I'm not really willing to go through the struggle we'd have to get there. Peter's quite happy to let me have control of everything because it means he doesn't have to do much thinking. He never wanted to be a parent in the first place, and I feel so much guilt that that's where I overcompensate and allow for his weaknesses because I think, 'How fair is this for me to expect him to be doing this properly when he really wasn't interested in doing it in the first place?'"

For his part, Peter soon realized what an important contribution Jon made to the household. One day, only half in jest, he asked LJ, "What did we do before we had Jon?"

Unorthodox though the arrangement is, it works. Some people find it odd and respond to the arrangement with surprise or shock or sometimes outright dismay. Nobody is neutral. According to LJ, some people can't believe it and are very curious. "Some people who've known us for a long time don't get it. For most people it was, 'How's Jon managing it?' Everyone was quite protective of Jon, and my family was, of course, quite protective of Peter because they still don't know why I ever left. I mean, he was the funny guy who did the dishes."

And then some people find the arrangement threatening because if it can work, then what does that say about the traditional way of doing things? "You get a bit of cold shoulder or an odd response," says LJ, "because they can't really support you when their own relationship is flawed and they're not doing anything about it, but you are."

Jon says that they themselves joke about the setup they've got. "We always say it's like a Jerry Springer situation. But I don't see it as something outrageous at all. It's something that works and that's all that matters. It doesn't really matter whether people like it or not."

LJ echoes his sentiment. "This won't be a forever thing, I would imagine. Peter takes the path of least resistance so until he's forced to do otherwise, he won't. And who knows, if ever I was to buy another house, I might make sure that it had a unit in it for Peter. That would be the ultimate, really, to have a place that had separate units . . . he'd have more privacy, we'd have more privacy, and he'd still be there. We all sacrifice a certain amount for the setup we have now, but no one's freaking out by any means. We all kind of accept it.

"There are moments where Sarah will come home and say, 'I'm having a sleepover in Daddy's room — we're watching the hockey game.' You can't buy that. She's in my house and she's with her dad and she's just happy, happy, happy. That's fantastic, just fantastic!" And that's what keeps everyone going, even on the challenging days.

CHAPTER NINE

A House Divided

"There was kind of a release and I cried
a lot, but I remember thinking, 'Oh, thank God I
don't have to do this anymore.'"

— Anna

TOM AND ANNA'S RELATIONSHIP ended in the space of a few minutes on the front porch of their house. He asked, "Do you want to end this?" She said, "Yes." And like a spent fire, their twenty-five year marriage was snuffed out.

There were no histrionics, no scenes, no cruel words. Their marriage had been dimming for a long time, and that fateful conversation had followed an uncharacteristically edgy weekend at Anna's family cottage. "I was cranky with Tom, which isn't like me," remembers Anna. "I was bitchy with him and he was snippy with me, and that's not how we work. We're non-confronters. We don't argue."

Their ability to maintain cordial relations had until then concealed a deeper truth: they had drifted apart and become emotionally estranged. Anna had not shared her thoughts or innermost feelings with Tom for a very long time, simply hiding that side of herself and tamping it down. "I think Tom saw me cry maybe five times in twenty-five years. I never expressed anything. I'd go into my bedroom and read. I certainly remember him coming up to the bedroom and saying, 'You can't just hide out here,' but that's what I was doing, hiding, because at the end of the day I didn't want to reveal anything."

To Tom, the fact that they had never argued was both a strength and a weakness — a strength because they'd raised five children in harmony, a weakness because their marriage had slowly faded. "I think we both felt that the marriage was in trouble, but we're great avoiders. I don't think we ever fought in our whole married life."

∽

Although Anna and Tom's love affair had cooled slowly, their courtship had burned very brightly. Anna remembers the time she first set eyes on Tom. She had just returned from three years at theater school in England and her sister was bringing her to a weekend of family festivities. On the way, Anna quizzed her about who would be there. "We have this huge family cottage. My mother used to invite up a bunch of architects [she worked with] from all across the country and Tom was one," said Anna. "It was this big family thing that had been going on for the three years I was away." Her sister told her about Tom, who was single at the time. He'd separated from his wife about eight months earlier and was raising two young children. Anna was in her early twenties, and curious about this "older man." She remembers being introduced to the group. "Tom just took his hat off and looked at me and I thought, 'Jesus, I hope that's the one who's single!'

"We flirted all weekend and I said to my mom, 'I think he might ask me out,' and she said, 'No, no, no way!' She thought I was going to go off and marry a Hollywood producer or something. Tom called, and we went out. We actually had a horrible first date." Anna says she probably would never have seen him again, but for some reason invited him in for coffee. "I don't know what it was, but the gods wanted us to be together somehow. . . It was like it was fated. We lived together almost immediately."

Anna found she had fallen into an instant family. She and Tom had custody of his son and daughter from his first marriage, and co-parenting kept them fully occupied. Anna remembers the challenges of those early days. "Their mom was pretty much in the picture, so the children went and saw her every other weekend." Tom had a good relationship with his ex-wife, and Anna gives him credit for that. "There could have been a lot of animosity. She'd left the kids, so she was having a hard time . . . going through a lot of turmoil. I heard him on the phone, so patient with her. She and I became friends, and she liked how I was with the kids. With the fusses she was making, it would have been so easy to get angry. Tom just said, 'I'm not going to do that to the kids.' He's a very good father. Kids come first, there's no question, and he's very involved in their lives — always has been."

Eventually, Tom and Anna decided to get married and have a baby of their own. They had a summer wedding, and fifteen months later, their son was born. At the time they agreed, Anna somewhat reluctantly, to have just one child. Tom was suffering a bit of parenting fatigue, which Anna could understand. But five years later, they had an "oops" pregnancy, and Anna discovered she was carrying twins. Their marriage had been unsteady, so it came at a bad time. According to Anna, Tom was in the middle of a mid-life crisis, re-thinking his work and his family life. She believes that if not for the twins, life might have unfolded quite differently. "It was a double whammy. He really didn't want to have another child and I don't blame him, because by this time his daughter was seventeen."

Although Tom had balked at the idea of having another child, when he heard there were two babies coming, things changed. "It was interesting," Anna says, "because he went, 'Oh, well, that really is going to make me stay.' He just turned around completely and was happy about it."

So they got on with raising five children. And for the better part of a decade, they did so quite compatibly. They were engaged and involved parents, which is why it was especially unsettling to both of them when their own relations began to fray. For other couples, a weekend of wrangling might have come with the territory, but for Anna and Tom, it ruptured the peace they'd assiduously maintained to mask tensions and dissatisfaction. When the fissures became obvious, they were compelled to examine the state of their marriage.

"We were just avoiding the issues," said Tom. "At the time they don't seem to be all that significant, and you chalk it up to having kids and busy lives." Looking back, he sees that while avoidance was a useful tactic, "We were both independently thinking, 'What if this doesn't work? How are we going to manage? If we did separate, what would we do? Would one of us leave?'"

Anna and Tom have very different personalities. She has a wide-open face and broad smile, and eyes that tell you that her brain is busy all the time. Tom is more buttoned down — compact, fit, self-contained. She needs a lot of buzz in her life and he's more self-sustaining. The course of their life together was not an unfamiliar one among couples. "We were like roommates," said Anna. "We were good at bringing up the kids together. We had just lost all intimacy in our relationship. I guess I had not loved him, or been in love with him, for a long time. There was such a distance between us that I sort of didn't trust him with who I was anymore. He's a compassionate person. . . but I just stopped talking to him about who I was and he didn't understand where I was at. My brain and heart go all over the place, where his are very steady and straightforward. He's a fixer, and I didn't want to be fixed, I needed a listener. So I started to pull away and rely on my friends for that kind of intimacy. It was definitely as much me as him pulling away."

Anna made herself so busy that she didn't have time to deal with the one relationship closest to her. She says she's not really a workaholic, but she remembers Tom going out and buying her champagne one day when he heard her say 'No' to somebody on the phone. "I just filled my life so I never had to think about it," she admits. "On the surface it looked really good because I was always into something and had an interesting life, but we'd go to bed and we were like strangers. I just hated the feeling. I remember once going away for this romantic weekend and saying to a therapist, 'It feels like I have to make love to this stranger, and yet he's not a stranger.' That's an awful, awful, awful feeling."

To their credit, they tried to hold the marriage together by seeking outside help, Tom recalls. "Part of the counseling was to take us through some exercises we could do on our own that would help strengthen the relationship. When we got on our own, though, we weren't doing it and so we began to ask ourselves, 'Why aren't we doing it? Why aren't we making that extra effort if we're really serious about this?'"

Any effort they did make turned to frustration and confusion as their efforts backfired. "I was committed to trying to make it work although I didn't feel anything," Anna confided. "Things were getting tenser rather than better, because we'd work on it when we went for therapy for a few days, and then it was really awful. We realized we were doing it for other people, not for us." As that reality sank in, each struggled in isolation with how to come to grips with the implications. Neither was ready to bail on the other, or their children, nor had it occurred to them to reinvent the tie between them. But slowly, they both began to see that they had to do something.

When Tom finally broached the idea of splitting up, Anna was anything but devastated. She felt relief. "I sensed that he was testing a little bit," says Anna. "I agreed, and I think that surprised him, although I can't say for sure, since we've never talked about that." She believes if she had suggested they keep trying and apologized for the weekend, he probably would have kept going. "I may be wrong," she says, "but I think I was more ready than he was."

Once they'd broken the silence, they were able to consider how to create a relationship that was closer to how they had come to feel about each other. "Trying to keep it together had been the hardest part," says Anna. "There was kind of a release, and I cried a lot, but I remember thinking, 'Oh, thank God I don't have to do this anymore.'"

At that point, figuring out what she *didn't* want was as important to Anna as what she *did* want. All around her, she had seen how others had dealt with crumbling relationships, and denial sometimes overrode the truth. "I've met a lot of women who know their marriage is a sham in terms of real intimacy," Anna said. "They fall in love with other people, but decide that the marriage is more important. I don't know how they do it. You think, 'I guess this is it' [instead of] being really alive and saying, 'Wait a minute! There's some life in the old gal yet!'"

But Anna had opened Pandora's box, and had felt the exhilaration of what life could be during a trip she'd taken to Cuba by herself some months earlier. "I had come alive down there. I really loved it and I felt so awakened. . . I realized how incredibly dead I was. My life was plodding and I wasn't happy. I tend to be a person who, once I know something, I just know it. And once I knew it was over, there was no question. There was no regret."

For them, separating was free of rancor or recrimination, but Tom was mindful of how the outside world views marriage breakdown. "I don't know why, but there seems to be a stigma attached to it . . . of some kind of failure, when in fact it was a developmental stage. Both of us realized that this relationship wasn't working and we both wanted to go in separate directions. It was in many ways a positive thing, but you feel kind of guilty, ashamed, whatever."

Luckily, neither felt a need to rush to a solution. They agreed in August to split up, but kept it secret until the following June, when the twins were finished elementary school. The children had been largely unaware of their parents' marital stresses. "For the kids, all seemed normal," Anna remembers. "They didn't see the slow, insidious disintegration." Keeping mum about their decision bought Anna and Tom time to begin planning for what would come next. They were on good terms, so making the transition in this way worked for them.

In the interim they made one change that was invisible to the outside world and explicable to the children. "We lived this kind of weird existence," says Tom, "where I moved out of our shared bedroom and into our guestroom. Anna had been having difficulty sleeping, insomnia and all that, so the kids were enquiring, 'Dad, why are you over there?' Without lying about it, we said, 'Well your mom's having difficulty sleeping, she's up late at night and she finds my snoring is keeping her awake.' They sort of bought that, it was fine, and the rest of our life was going on pretty normally."

❧

As they played with ideas about what to do next, the layout of their house provided a solution they felt they could live with. "I knew both of us were very interested in being with the kids, and being involved in parenting," Tom explains. "We were fortunate that our house had a separate apartment. When we bought the place, one of the appeals was that the apartment could be used by my mother or Anna's mom as they got older. At the time it was being rented out, but the tenants wouldn't be there forever. In my mind, that became a possibility. I wouldn't have to live far away and could be close to the kids with minimal disruption of their lives. That was uppermost in my thinking and when we started talking about it, it was uppermost in Anna's."

Serendipitously, the tenants bought a house and moved out, leaving the apartment empty at just the right time. It was small, but it could work. Anna and the kids stayed in the big house, which had five bedrooms, and Tom moved into the apartment, where he had an office, a bedroom, a kitchen, and a bathroom. The apartment was connected to the house by a door, but neither Tom nor Anna felt a need to create strict divisions between themselves. The kids' lives carried on as usual, sometimes in the main house, sometimes in Tom's place. Their computers were at Tom's, and he continued to use the kitchen and family room in the main house.

Tom's presence in her part of the house didn't bother Anna at all. "It's the way we were living for a long time anyway, but we didn't have to be worried about the relationship," she says. She also recognized her own financial vulnerability. "It's been great because Tom's taken care of most of the costs. I have my bills and my car, and I take care of the phone bill, but Tom, rather than paying child support, has taken care of all the kids' stuff here, and the house and the food. I was really appreciative of the fact that I wasn't sitting in a small apartment somewhere trying to pay my rent at this point in my life. I had never been out there making a living. I had kids from the time I met him, right out of theater school — two little kids around that weren't mine, and then more. We had brought up five kids, and I was in the position where I wasn't the main moneymaker."

Anna and Tom began to operate more autonomously, but family life continued much as usual. Tom remembers, "We no longer sat and discussed what we were going to do with our lives, or even with our week, you know? We just did it and told the other one what we were doing and tried to arrange it in such a way that one of us was covering. Often we were both here and we'd still have family dinners and prepare dinner together."

When it came time to reveal what they'd kept hidden for so many months, both Anna and Tom had a tough time lifting the cloak of secrecy. The hardest part was telling the kids. They were all shocked because Anna and Tom got along so well. "They had lived with this kind of friendly surface, and we always respected each other," Anna says. "We explained that we felt like marriage wasn't going to work anymore. We'd gone to therapy and we'd been trying to work it out, but we'd decided that we didn't want to do that anymore."

Tom's offspring from his first marriage were grown and had moved away by the time he and Anna made their situation known, but their son Matthew was only fifteen when they sat him down to explain. Matthew had always wrestled with behavioral issues, so Anna and Tom were very worried about how he might react. "He was amazing actually, for him," Anna remembers. "This could have been a great opportunity for him to have one of his attention-getting things. He did act out later, but at the time, he was very reasonable and said, 'Well, if that's what you two have decided, I trust you that it's what you need to do.'"

The twins, Nick and Sam, were ten, and had distinctly different reactions. "Sam is very honest and expressive. She's articulate, so she could express her pain, and there was a lot of pain for her. I remember the hardest part was when she was lying in bed and she said, 'I just want this to be different. I want it all to go away . . . but I want you to be happy too and that's the most important thing.' She's an amazing kid, but I remember that desperateness of her wishing we had never said that. It killed me because I know that feeling. It's like, 'Make this a nightmare and go away.'

"And poor Nick was always the quiet one who never articulated anything. He sort of grunted and went and watched TV, which is his modus operandi for everything. I realized that I had to watch him really carefully, because he is a deep feeler. He never says what he feels. So whatever happened, Sam would articulate it and I would know that was what Nick would be feeling too. Sam would say, 'I need to spend time with you, Mom, or 'I need to be with you more,' and I would immediately apply it to Nick and realize he needs this too, because he would never ask."

Tom was distressed that he wasn't able to insulate the children from pain. "You realize it is having an impact on them and you're sorry about that, but were we better to stay together, unhappy, in a relationship for their sake? Initially their reaction was that one of us would take off, even though we said we wouldn't. My older son is quite verbal and he was cool about it. Of the twins, my daughter was quite outspoken about it. The boy was more sensitive, and I've always felt that he was much more upset and hurt, but never really expressed much. We've tried to talk to him about it and he's not really interested in exploring that right now."

Children have an uncanny ability to intuit the truth of a situation. Anna had been completely caught off guard by her older son's insights. Long before they'd decided to separate, or had even paid attention to the downhill slide of their marriage, Mathew had understood what was going on between his parents. "I remember him being a barometer. He said, 'You guys do nothing with your emotional life,' and we're going, 'But we get along well.' He is a mightily sensitive kid and he could see right through our not arguing. Kids sense it."

Once the shock of their parents' revelation diminished and the children had some time to adjust, they began to see that their world was going to continue much as it always had. "They all had their own schedules, a lot of the time they weren't around anyway, so they'd come and go. But the fact that there was a parent here was always reassuring for them."

The arrangement made sense for everyone and both Anna and Tom knew why they were doing it in the way they were. "I never felt like I compromised much," Tom remembers. "You obviously do in any relationship, but I was certainly free to choose, and it so happened we both chose to stay here and not alter our lives all that much."

Tom also wanted to continue being a hands-on parent, as he had been with all of his children. He wasn't particularly keen on repeating his own parents' example — doing their duty, but from a distance. Tom had also observed some patterns he wasn't fond of among men who were peers, and of a younger generation. "I'm amazed, when I see young couples now, how a lot of guys still aren't pulling their share or taking much interest other than taking the kid off to hockey or dance once in a while. They think that's the extent of their responsibility."

Tom felt fortunate to be able to continue to parent and share a role. He wanted to be part of their day-to-day lives.

"To have an equal role in the parenting means, okay, you've got to make concessions and you've got to sit down and work these things out, otherwise you're going to be standing outside looking in. It's not going to work unless the two of you can come to some kind of agreement on how to share these responsibilities."

And the benefits for grownups and children alike were palpable. "Anna's family is still very friendly towards me, inviting me up to their family cottage and the rest of it, so I haven't felt ostracized or left out. This summer I went up with my new partner and Anna wasn't there. I was there with the aunts and uncles, and the kids love that extended family situation. Had we gone our separate ways and had more animosity or division, I'm sure her family would have felt almost obliged to take sides, to somehow exclude me or certainly not welcome me as much. All of those kinds of associations are important to the kids and I think that's what they lose out on in relationships that are more fractious, that really get physically divided. Who can choose between their mom and dad. . . or their mom's family and their dad's family?"

Still there's a tradeoff with an arrangement like this. What's gained in family involvement is lost in privacy. It was a deal worth making, according to Tom. His apartment became the center of activity for the kids. "I moved my office over but it has three computers with MSN and e-mail and their school projects. They no sooner get home from school and they're in there. For a time, Anna was using the computers, so my office isn't *my* space." He didn't mind, and at the end of the day, the one spot that was his, where he could retreat and shut the door, was his bedroom. That space was sacrosanct. Otherwise, there was a lot of backing and forthing between both domains.

Kitchens are often the locus of family dramas. As with so many other couples, this was true for Anna and Tom, but in an interesting twist, the kitchen was one room they chose to continue sharing. Cooking had become a source of contention, according to Tom, but in his view, any quarrels about their different styles of grocery shopping and views about how a pantry should be stocked overlaid the real issue, which was money. Anna agrees. "Money? It's the biggest tension we had," she admits. "We were always running over on our overdraft, and I thought a lot of it had to do with food," Tom says. He used to complain about it but eventually realized that if he didn't like it, he should do it himself. "She never said that but I concluded that, so I do the grocery shopping now. The kids complain about the lack of goodies and stuff in the house because I tend to buy more simply than she used to. Anna wasn't offended giving that up; I think she was relieved not to have the responsibility of doing the shopping."

Anna has no trouble understanding Tom's frustration with her spending habits. "I'm terrible with money and he's very frugal. I have it, I spend it. I'm really generous with my money. If I can buy you a present, I buy you a present." Tom was prepared to continue being the main income generator for the family, but he had to secure an agreement from Anna. He took control of their finances, and she handed it over. "I let go. I could fight about things, but in many ways I realize that it doesn't matter. It's not important. When it came down to it, he had control of the money really, because I'm just not a financially secure person. We separated our bank accounts so I couldn't go into our mutual account and go and buy things. That just seemed fair and reasonable. I don't feel anger about it. I feel frustration at my own self, that I'm not independently financially viable yet."

❦

In spite of the necessity for a more formal understanding about money, life in their house was otherwise unmediated. Neither was inclined to institute formal rules. Trust was implicit between them, and that was enough. "I was responsible for maintaining the residence, which involves food and running the house, until such time as we decided to sell the house and go our separate ways," Tom says. "Typical of our married and unmarried life, none of this was really carved in stone . . . the division of labor is understood. We have sorted out a pattern that is acceptable to both of us."

Anna and Tom developed new routines so they'd have a modicum of independence and still get the kids to their swim meets and school functions. Since they'd also begun to date other people, they had to figure out some way to accommodate the need for "time off." The logistics fell into place relatively easily, but since designing their new life was like making a puzzle without a picture to guide them, it took some experimenting. Eventually they figured out the kind of schedules that made sense for them. "We kept having to negotiate. 'Are you going to be out tonight or am I going to be out tonight?' We were never both out," explains Anna. They agreed that every second weekend, one would have from Friday until Sunday night off.

There were some strains, of course, but they'd put in place an arrangement that was sturdy enough to withstand the pressures of day-to-day living. When there were hiccups in the schedule, they were flexible with each other. Tom knows that when he feels hard done by, he may not be the only one. "I find if I just shut up about it and don't complain, when I'm letting down my side she'll pick up the slack and not complain about it. Some would say it's just part of our avoidance that we don't sit down and map it out, but there hasn't been a whole lot of friction. We're both fairly easygoing, so it hasn't been a big issue. I'm sure with a lot of couples, though, it would definitely help to sit down and sort out how the division is going to occur."

Once they went public with their news, Anna took flak from people who didn't understand what they were doing. Why, they wondered, would she leave a marriage that was "good enough"? "People certainly said, 'If you can get along, why don't you?' I got that a lot. When I say, 'Well, he's a great guy and I still love him, you know. I love him as a person,' they say, 'Why would you do that, then? I know what you're feeling, but I would never leave my family.' I say, 'Well, I haven't left my family. I've just admitted the truth of the marriage.'" Anna doesn't take umbrage at these enquiries. "I get it. I could have chosen to live that lie, and it wouldn't have been as horrible as if I had been in a marriage where he was beating me, or was abusive to me. I could have done that, but I would have died inside."

For Tom it was bureaucratic frustrations that baffled and annoyed him. "The income tax department has great difficulty because we don't have two separate addresses, even though the apartment is a legally acknowledged one. It was, from a property appraisal point of view, shown as a separate apartment, and that was what I had to document and give to them. I thought, 'There must be other people like this, still living in the same house but who've created an upstairs apartment and downstairs apartment. Nominate a third party and have them do an audit of the house to see if it's physically separated. The door's always open, but we are living apart and not conjugally.'"

The tax episode wasn't an isolated incident. Tom remembers several instances where people were openly incredulous about what they were doing. "My accountant always asks if Anna and I are still together and he just shakes his head. I remember when I first told him about our arrangement, he said, 'Good luck, but I'll have to be honest, I don't think this is going to work, Tom.' The next year I'd come in with my returns and he'd ask me, 'Still working?' And then he'd say, 'I've been through so many bitter, acrimonious fights, I just find it amazing that you guys are able to do it.' And other people . . . I was talking to Anna's lawyer when we started proceedings with the divorce. I thought maybe somebody should have power of attorney. So I talked to her lawyer, and she asked me who I was thinking of. And I said, 'Well, I was thinking maybe Anna' and she looked at me and said, 'Well, *that's* unusual.' Every once in a while you get people who react that way."

To be fair, it's not a huge stretch to see why people weren't quite sure what to make of how Anna and Tom were living. To a world familiar with break-ups mired in acrimony, it was a bit of a mind-bender. Sometimes they surprised even themselves. They had stopped confiding in each other while married but found they had things to talk about once they had separated. Tom remembers with some amusement how this new intimacy really flummoxed outsiders. "We've developed into really good friends. We talk about our lives together. At one time we were both dating and we would sit at breakfast and share stories about the troubles we were having with our current date or whatever. You talk to other people and they think you're crazy."

Anna remembers this too. "The first time he came to me and said, 'I'm thinking of doing this and I don't know that my girlfriend will be very happy. What do you think?' I said, 'You're asking me for love advice? I can't believe this!' So I gave it to him. And why not? He trusted me enough to have a good answer."

❧

Tom was the first to begin going out with other people. Anna laughs at the memory of his first forays into dating. "I'd say it was within eight months, even though he swore to celibacy and he was never going to marry. That lasted a very short time. A single man in this town is like gold. The women were just flocking around him."

Anna found that, in the beginning, she had to deal with a few twinges of something that felt oddly like jealousy. "I had been away, and I came back and I think the twins told me, 'Dad's got a girlfriend.' Each phase we go through is always weird. I would have to re-adjust everything to get so that it became normal. I was more jealous of the relationship that he had with someone else than I was about him being with someone."

Anna and Tom had, in a sense, exited their marriage cleanly. Both wanted out, there had been no betrayal and no heartbreak. So, even if there were some uncomfortable transition periods, it was possible to ease into a new reality without hostility. This was particularly important when that reality included new partners. "The fact that she's dating somebody doesn't bring up any jealousy with me," Tom said. "I've let go. She's her own person. I don't have any feelings that way about her." But, however benign Tom's feelings had become toward his ex, he wasn't sure he'd have been quite so sanguine if another person had come too close. "I don't know how it would have worked if another partner had moved in with one of us, or both of us. Quite honestly — though I like to see myself as being fairly easygoing and liberal — to have another guy living in this house probably wouldn't have worked."

For their own reasons, new partners usually kept their

distance. "In many ways I think it's harder on others," Tom observed. "Obviously we've sorted out the arrangements between the two of us and feel quite comfortable with it, but it's difficult for the other person to buy into. The fear is you are still sleeping together, or you still have feelings towards one another. The assumption is that it could happen, given the fact that we're still physically here together. You try to reassure them that we're happy going our separate ways."

Those reassurances were often less successful than they might have hoped, according to Tom. "The people we were seeing had great difficulty with our relationship. Neither of them wanted to come into the house. If we had separated in the traditional way they would have felt much more comfort- able. But the lady I was seeing felt this was still 'our' home." Tom says Anna's boyfriend felt he was encroaching on another man's territory. "Her boyfriend eventually came over for some special dinners, but otherwise wouldn't set foot into the house. He felt this was still my domain."

So, to accommodate people's sensitivities, new love affairs were conducted somewhere other than in Tom and Anna's shared world. "It just so happened that the people we saw had their own places, which was good in a way because it got you out of the house, got you away," said Tom. "If Anna had a date and they were going to be out late or if she was going to stay over or something, she'd let me know and I would make sure that I was here."

Anna remembers one of the more ridiculous moments that she looks back on with some mirth. "It was a Father's

Day, and the kids phoned and said, 'Will you help us make dinner for Dad?' I gave up something I was doing downtown and I came home and we were preparing dinner together, the three of us. We were having a great time, laughing, and Tom came home with his girlfriend. They were out in the backyard, drinking martinis, while I was making dinner for him, and I thought there was something definitely wrong with this picture. I said to the kids, 'I don't need to be at dinner. I'm sorry, you're going to have to deal with this, because I don't want to deal with it.' And then I thought I was being totally childish, so I sat through the dinner. And as soon as dinner was over I went upstairs. That was one of those situations where you have to make up the rules. I think that's the thing, you're making up rules as you go."

A few months after Tom started dating, Anna began an intense relationship with an artist. He was eccentric and Anna found him compelling and confounding. His marriage had also ended, and he was juggling his own schedule with kids so their family lives overlapped very little. When he left her after eighteen months, Anna was devastated. It took her ages to pick up the pieces, which she did very slowly. The end of that relationship was a stark contrast to the end of her marriage. "When we broke up, I just wanted to die. I thought that was it, that was the last relationship I'd ever have, and I blew it. I was in such agony over losing this man that I had to look at myself really closely."

She began to recover, and as she did, she went through what she describes as a kind of spiritual awakening. "I want to create my own life. I think that's why I'm not meeting anybody right now. I want to know myself in the world alone, totally alone. It's given me such peace to know that I will never *need* a relationship. I know that I'm okay on my own, so I wouldn't stay in a relationship that is not healthy for me, or that doesn't bring me joy.

"I don't even know that I'd want a marriage again," Anna continues. I would love to have somebody that I felt really close to, that I could be with, but I would always want to be independent now. I've learned a lot about loneliness and being alone and realized that I was lonelier then than I am now, even though I had to go through a hoop to realize that loneliness takes form in many, many ways. I'm not frightened of loneliness anymore or of being alone."

While Anna's heart was mending, she had to contend with the rest of her life, which for a while looked bleak too. "I didn't have any work, and I ended up working in a coffee shop, which gave me all the time in the world to really look at myself. Nothing was coming my way, nothing, So I started walking, and I walked and hiked everywhere. I was just obsessive. But I wouldn't change a thing. I don't think there's anything that I would change. I'm going on the Camino de Santiago, an eight-hundred-kilometer walk across Spain, to figure out what happens now. I can't wait to get that backpack on my back and just go, 'Ah! That is over, I don't have to do this anymore.'"

Tom began his own journey too. He decided to head to Malaysia to help in the wake of the tsunami. Once the twins had gone off to school, and all of their children had been safely fledged, he and Anna sold their house, freeing each of them to re-invent themselves. "We're in a position where our lives are uncertain as to what the future holds, which is frightening on the one hand, but exciting on the other," he says. "You can do anything, whatever happens to come along. We're both in a situation now where we can entertain some pretty radical life changes. I think we're kind of looking forward to that."

Anna is proud of the example she and Tom have set for their children. She remembers being very impressed with the way her daughter handled a love affair that had spent itself. "I think in many ways, we've taught them a good lesson — that things do change. Love changes and love grows, and for some people it lasts longer than others, but you've got to be who you are. You've got to be on your own journey. You can't say 'forever.'"

The truth of this became crystal clear to her when a close friend was dealt a harsh lesson. "I had a girlfriend — young woman, thirty — who was madly, madly in love. They were going to get married. And one day he died. . . just died. They still don't know why. And she's struggling with, 'What was that about? If life can change that much, is it worth even trying to build anything?' Of course, I'm on the outside. . . [but yes,] it is, because what you had was so amazing, and you were lucky to have had that time. That's what I want my kids to know — enjoy it and love it and be totally there for the person. But be sure that you don't *need* that person, that you only *want* that person. There's such a difference between those two words."

At the end of their "experiment," Tom is clear-eyed about what made their efforts valuable. "What's going to minimize the disruption or inconvenience for the kids in terms of them moving around and yet accommodate your individual needs? If you can agree on that as the objective of this exercise, then you sit down and negotiate. I think what goes wrong with most miserable divorces is that what's good for the kids gets totally forgotten and it becomes what's good for me and how can I get back at my spouse? So if you can turn the equation around and put the focus on the kids and say, 'Okay, what are we going to do to minimize that disruption?' and work it back from there, then what we're doing isn't that unusual."

CHAPTER TEN

Reconcilable Differences

"I've stopped telling Joe how he should
feel about things and he's stopped letting me
do it. I don't storm off in a huff and
he doesn't shrug off my concerns. Most
of the time it works."

— Cate

MY MARRIAGE ENDED one cold January night, over dinner at
a bustling Greek restaurant. Joe and I had been to a parent-
teacher meeting at our son's high school and had decided to
catch a quick dinner afterwards. Over plates of Greek salad
and souvlaki, I blurted out what had been on my mind for
months. "Either we go into therapy or I will end this marriage."
Disbelief clouded his face. I had raised the subject before, but
this was the first time he seemed to really hear me. "You're
kidding," he said. A feeling of shock settled over our table,
and the air became still.

Joe and I have never had a lot in common. We move at

different speeds. He ambles; I hurtle. He's an "on the one hand, on the other hand" Libra; I'm a rototiller Leo. He listens to the Ramones; I like Handel. He's a Type-B artist; I'm a Type-A media producer. We met in 1985 at a local farmer's market, where, over back bacon sandwiches, I was breaking off a romance with a colleague of Joe's from the studio where they worked. Oblivious to the drama, Joe wandered over to chat and I was immediately intrigued. He was funny and handsome, with a brilliant smile.

Two weeks later, I asked him out. He was too shy to call me. On our first date, a hurried lunch at a greasy spoon, he spread pictures of his nieces on the table, and spoke lovingly about each one. We had dinner the next weekend at a tiny restaurant where we talked until the staff began sweeping up around us. When we walked under a full moon to the beach, I was completely smitten. I had been married to a cad who had cheated and lied, so I was on high alert for knavish men, but Joe was the opposite, with an honesty and sweetness that made me trust him. Within months, he had moved into my small apartment. We began to collide with each other early on (he once tried to tell me how to cut a cucumber properly, and I didn't take kindly to the instruction), but our shared sense of humor helped us survive even our testiest moments.

After a few years, we bought a dilapidated Victorian row house in a then-unfashionable neighborhood near a downtown mental hospital. The house needed work, and the process of renovating was riddled with conflict. We never could agree about house stuff. When we went to choose wallpaper for our dining room, I wanted a heritage pattern and he wanted primary colors. The strain between us was so palpable that the shop clerk asked if we'd like to cool off in a corner with a cup of tea.

In 1988, when I was 32, I discovered I was pregnant. This was a much-wanted baby, but I was reluctant to marry again. We finally succumbed to family pressure, and six weeks before our son's due date we were married by a judge in her chambers at City Hall. I wore black and insisted only our grandmothers attend as witnesses, and by the time we drove off for our honeymoon, my feet were so swollen from the pregnancy that we had to stop to buy me some size 11 tennis shoes.

Our son, Jake, was born in late December, and Joe and I soon lost ourselves in the business and busyness of raising him — washing cloth diapers and doing daily daycare runs. Four years later I became pregnant again, and since our tiny house couldn't hold another person, we bought a roomy five-bedroom semi in Toronto's west end just before our daughter arrived. Maddie was a shy baby who for the first three months of her life clung to me like the tendrils of a vine.

We were an unlikely pair, Joe and I, but I cherished his kindness and his humor and appreciated that he was a fully engaged dad — so engaged that we once had a protracted debate about whether our toddler should be eating a peanut butter and banana sandwich (my choice) or the "hot and hearty" meal Joe thought his child should be getting. I believed I had virtue and truth on my side and so did he.

For many years Joe gave me comic strips as gifts — depictions of our life together, scenes of domestic bliss, discord, hilarity, and angst. In each strip, there was always one frame portraying me with my jaw cranked open and daggers flying out of my mouth, headed in Joe's general direction. I loved the way those comic strips chronicled our flawed union, and I framed them all and hung them in our kitchen. They were overstated caricatures, but they told a truth about the stormy relationship my mother-in-law called our "funny little marriage." It *was* "funny," but for a long time we were able to brush off our differences.

We never waged all-out marital war, but we had constant border skirmishes that I used to call our "lettuce and laundry

wars." We'd argue about the kind of produce I bought or how he made the bed. The washer and dryer became the locus of friction as we disagreed about color sorting and wrinkle control. He didn't see the need for either, and I was committed to both. We were so at odds about domestic issues that I sometimes said to him, only half joking, that we should move into side-by-side duplexes with a dial on each door that we could spin to indicate whether the other spouse was welcome to visit ("Come on in" or "Maybe later").

Eventually our differences became too significant to laugh off. We lost the habit of conversation, and disaffection settled in. Every time we tried to broach the problem, it was like striking steel on flint. I would talk and talk to keep the sadness at bay; he'd climb to his third-floor studio and bury his feelings in his work, drawing for hours on end. Or he'd sit in the family room, watching film noir videos and folding huge piles of wrinkled sheets and towels. I'd lie in bed, looking glumly over the footboard at a wall of family pictures, feeling trapped and hopeless.

We weren't a car-wreck of a marriage, but we were stuck in cruise control. I knew we were in serious trouble when our ten-year-old daughter would jump in to mediate as we bickered about something minor — like whether to have pasta or chicken for dinner. Looking at her earnest little face across the kitchen one night, I thought, "Things have gone too far." But if we split up, what would happen to our family?

ᔕ

I began therapy and implored Joe to join me. He wasn't ready yet, and by the time he visited the therapist, the "we" that used to be was over. I felt we'd gone as far as we could as a couple, but I had no idea how we could dissolve our couple-life without jettisoning our family-life. We had inhabited our relationship for almost two decades and I didn't know how to take it apart and rebuild. We both struggled.

The central concern for each of us was the kids. Early on, we made one pledge: our children were not going to become cannon fodder in any of our battles. One friend who'd gone through a hideous divorce, and plowed all his money into fighting with his ex-wife, encouraged us to "keep our eyes on the prize" — meaning the children. We knew where we didn't want to go, if not exactly where we were headed. We knew that although we may have been lousy as a married couple, we were good at other stuff. We were partners in the slog of everyday life, and we were great co-parents. We were almost always in agreement about how to raise our children, and tensions in that area were always surface, not profound.

I trusted that we both wanted to preserve what was good between us but get rid of what didn't work, and gradually I found myself trying to imagine what might be possible. Joint parenting was our bottom line. But could we do better? We shared a vague sense that we wanted something other than a "one week on, one week off" routine. Also, there were financial concerns. We had lived within our means, but we were mortgage-poor. Joe and I would each have even less trying to go it alone. Was there some way to stay together geographically but split up emotionally? Since our marriage had always been a little outside the box, why couldn't our separation?

The first few months after our watershed discussion over dinner, we stumbled around while we continued to live together, keeping our decision from our kids. It was hard. I used to sit for hours in front of the fireplace in our living room, musing about how to reconfigure our marriage without nuking the entire family. Joe would sometimes stop on his way to the third floor and we'd talk to each other over the stair railing. Some very delicate conversations took place while he lingered by the newel post and I sat curled up on the couch.

Therapy became a big part of patching together a new reality. The first time I sat in the psychologist's warm, book-lined office on the second floor of her house, I was bristling with anger. A slender, elegant woman, Sheila would fold her long frame into a black leather chair and listen as I poured out my grievances, then challenge me to remember what had drawn me to Joe, even though I resisted. She wanted me to deal with the whole person I had loved, not the two-dimensional man I'd created in my anger, and she asked me to try to envision some kind of future for us instead of brooding about our failings.

She prodded me to think about the kind of person I wanted to be once we had finished our marital makeover, and I often squirmed at having to revise myself as well as our family. But I trusted her method and bit by bit I moved forward, as did Joe, who began to see her on his own. I truly believe she was the midwife to our emerging new relationship.

We had to redraw our emotional boundaries and learn how to be nicer to each other. Sometimes that was unsettling. One day, in a fit of temper, I confronted Joe outside his studio and he sent me on my way, asking me to come back when I'd settled down. I realized Sheila had taught him that he didn't have to engage with me if we were at odds, and as he quietly closed the door in my face, I spluttered all the way down the stairs, cursing our therapist for teaching him to take control.

∻

While Joe and I discussed ways to reconfigure our family, I began to hear about others who had attempted atypical arrangements. In one case, a couple had bought houses kitty-corner from each other, and they and their new partners and all the kids ate together several times a week. Another couple had continued to work together after their separation and live in the same house, new partners coming and going. Every story bolstered my confidence in the possibility of pioneering something new.

And reinventing our life and our space was like pioneering: lots of possibilities, lots of pitfalls. Should we buy two little houses near each other (very expensive) or two condos in the same building, maybe on the same floor? Going through this mental exercise was almost fun for me because I've always been a bit of a real estate junkie, buying and redecorating houses in my head. But change does not come as easily for Joe, and the process, for him, was very stressful. We finally settled on a basic plan: one way or another we would share a space where we could co-parent but still live separate lives. We decided it was time to tell the kids.

On a June afternoon, with the late-day sun spilling across the black-and-white tile floor of the kitchen, we asked the kids to sit with us at the table. "Daddy and I have something to discuss with you," I said. The minute our daughter realized what was coming, her face crumpled and she ran to hide at the back of the coat closet. Our son, who was then fourteen, struggled to maintain his composure, and just one tear rolled down his cheek during the conversation. Many times they asked us why. Why did we have to do this? We tried to explain that we had grown out of being married partners but that we would never stop being a team when it came to raising them. In all the years I've been a parent, this was the only time I felt that I'd betrayed my children's trust. They knew divided families where the children bore the brunt of their parents' failed relationship, and it would be a long time before they believed that Joe and I would still be friends, that we'd remain united as parents, and that we'd all stay together.

I enlisted the help of a real estate agent who knew every-thing about the market in our neighborhood. She hauled me out to look at every place that might have potential, and I traipsed through more grotty houses than I cared to count. It was demoralizing. We toyed with the idea of staying in our house and dividing it into two apartments. We even talked to an architect friend who spent hours with us, helping us rethink our space over spaghetti and cheap wine. The truth was, while we were discussing walls and windows, we were actually figuring out how to redesign a family.

Then, in October, the real estate agent called to insist that we see a house she'd found just a few blocks over on a tree-lined street, a lovely old matron of a place from the 1920s, already divided nicely into four apartments. We knew from the minute we walked in the front door that it was meant for us. Joe could have the apartment on the second floor, which had a studio, and I could have the apartment on the ground floor. Our son would have a bedroom in Joe's apartment, and our daughter would have one in mine, and they would float between us. We'd find tenants for the basement and the third-floor apartments. Joe and I could have the privacy we needed, but we could all stay together.

We went home and did the math. With the rental units to help defray the cost, we could just afford it. In a matter of days we made an offer and put our old place up for sale. It seemed ironic that, in the midst of separating, we were moving up in the real estate market, assuming more debt and becoming landlords.

ᥴᠵᢀ

Our families and many of our friends thought we'd cracked up. Some reacted with astonishment or dismay and some with envy. Doubters took us aside and pointed out potential pitfalls. At one family party, nobody seemed to know quite how to deal with us, and one fellow we knew chatted amicably with me for a long while, but sidled up to Joe the moment I left and advised him to "lawyer up." Our own lawyer asked us if we were sure we knew what we were doing.

Two of the couples we were closest to were so rattled by our undertaking that they didn't know how to behave if they couldn't choose sides. I had to take them to dinner and exact a promise that they'd trust us to know what we were doing. We didn't know, of course, but we were slogging hard to move in the right direction and those friends have since become our staunchest allies. Luckily, we had cheerleaders, too. Once our parents and siblings were onside, their support was solid and generous, even if some were perplexed by how we might accomplish our goal.

On the day we signed the final mortgage papers at our kitchen table, the bottom of my stomach fell out, and I remember looking at Joe to see if he was as terrified as I was. He was. But it was one of those moments when you hold your breath and jump.

In preparing for the move, we each had to choose what we wanted to keep and get rid of the rest. Shopping had been my anodyne, and our house was jammed full of memorabilia and antique furniture I'd collected. Joe didn't want the armoires or antiques. He wanted to divest himself of the things that had come to represent — for him — the failure of what we had been. In the end, nineteen station wagon loads of castoffs went from our house to a charity.

Getting ready to move was one of the most stressful times of my life. As usual, our pace was different. I packed quickly and Joe packed — well, methodically. He wanted to throw things out; I wanted to hang on to stuff. Eventually we learned to divide up the work and stay in different rooms on different floors, but it took every lesson learned in therapy and every ounce of will to avoid defaulting to toxic behavior.

Articulating how I feel is the way I choose to work my way through pain, but Joe is a man of few words and humor is the balm for his soul. At about this time, I could tell that he was beginning to repair emotionally. He developed what he called "the Freedom Dance," and as a demonstration of how he was going to feel about not being my husband anymore, he'd stab the air with his arms and leap around like an aging rock star, singing, "Freedom, freeedom, freeeeedom." This would send people into hysterics, and while I was glad he was able to see the upside of our demise, my feelings took a little bruising when he did it once too often.

The new house required some cosmetic work: new carpets, paint, and fixtures. My mother became our "consul-tant," spending time with every member of the family to help them envision their new space, sleeping in the empty house on a lumpy cot, and overseeing the painters and contractors. Together, she and Joe designed his apartment, which evolved as a "not-Cate" space, and as I saw him exercising his very different taste, I felt like cheering for him. In our other life, he had surrendered control over the domestic world to me, but now he was able to pick whatever tile and carpet he wanted for his new apartment. His place became a cheerful palette of blues, greens, and yellows, while mine retained the earthy shades I loved so much. Our daughter pored over color charts with my mother, choosing a pumpkin orange for her walls, while our son requested custom shelving in his room for his beloved computer and stereo. The move gave us all a chance to imagine a new and different future.

Thirteen months after my dinner-time ultimatum, a moving van pulled up to the house at 6:45 on a cold February morning. It was a day of small sadnesses. My mother-in-law arrived at our old house in mid-afternoon, when it looked empty and forlorn, and stood looking at the shell where our kids had been babies, where we'd celebrated birthdays and High Holidays and hung stockings on the mantel at Christmas. We'd lost something she had also loved, and she looked so disappointed. But I felt enormous relief. Being alone in my own space was intoxicating, and the first night in my new apartment, I closed my door and collapsed onto the sofa, repeating the word "mine!" like a mantra. I sensed that although we were still tied so closely, we had given ourselves and each other the gift of independence.

❧

It took a few months to establish new routines. Joe and I each have our own kitchens so we take turns with lunch and dinner duty. Our doors are never locked, and the kids roam between the two apartments. When I'm not home, our daughter sleeps upstairs in her dad's apartment. Our son, who has now moved out on his own, used to wander down to my kitchen rooting for food at all hours, often clad in nothing but his boxer shorts. There's a clear division of our households, but also lots of overlap. For us, that works well. It allows us to participate equally in our children's lives while helping each other with the mundane details of daily life. We share our little mutt, Cola, and she sleeps wherever she wants. We created a system of being on and off duty, taking turns doing dinner or making lunches, ferrying the kids to music lessons and getting them to doctors' appointments. We trade off responsibility for weekends, confer regularly about our schedules, and share our parenting responsibilities in a way that gives each of us a lot of flexibility. We communicate a lot via phone now, but early on we had intercom units that sat on the kitchen counter in each apartment, and most mornings there'd be a buzz at around 7:45. "Good morning. You guys up yet? Can I send Cola down?" The dog would come bouncing down the stairs and park herself at my front door until I let her out into the garden for a morning pee. She still does. Thousands of minor decisions were negotiated over those little speakers, everything from making sure school forms had been signed to extending a spontaneous dinner invite.

Over the years, there have been times when we've had to work hard to maintain a balance within our unusual family. We discovered that potentially explosive issues are sometimes better resolved in writing than in person, so e-mail is our mediator. We've sent each other hundreds of missives over the last few years and used the good disaster prevention tactic that a friend once taught me: never push the Send button on a contentious message until you've stopped to breathe and reflect on the impact your words might have on the recipient.

However, we've also learned to listen carefully to each other, and to trust that we will back each other up. We are, in a lurching kind of way, beginning to change old patterns of interacting. I've stopped telling Joe how he should feel about things, and he's stopped letting me do it. I don't storm off in a huff, and he doesn't shrug off my concerns. Most of the time it works. For the rest, we do what we've had lots of practice doing: we apologize when we are in the wrong. That's something we were always good at; no matter how infantile or petulant our behavior, we always knew how to say that we were sorry.

❧

Throughout this process, we've taken great pains to explain to the children that we are committed to working things out when we disagree, and over time they've seen us wrestle with some perplexing and difficult situations. Our arrangement demands that the adults behave like grownups, even if they're not feeling particularly mature about things, and I've learned from this experience the importance of empathy for the other characters in our domestic drama. We do have moments when we push each other's buttons, and familiar demons whisper in our ears from time to time, but we're getting better at recognizing them before they wreak havoc on our state of calm.

There have definitely been moments where the kids have been frustrated or frightened or downright angry with one or both of us. Our daughter hates it if we have a less than convivial discussion and tries to intervene if she senses any tension between us. We've had to explain that disagreements don't necessarily signal an impending storm. She's just beginning to believe that she doesn't have to act as her father's protector. Our son has a different temperament. Like many teenage boys, he holds his emotional cards close to his chest, and he has always taken things in stride. Recently my daughter confided to me that she'll always wish we had stayed married, but if we *had* to break up, she's glad we did it the way we did. My son has told me the same thing. Neither of our children could possibly have understood what a gift they were giving with those words.

The kids have taken turns testing the solidarity of our arrangement in their own ways, checking to see what they might get away with. Our son once tried to pull a fast one over curfew times, playing Joe and me off against each other. The three of us had a spontaneous meeting on neutral ground, the stairs between Joe's place and mine, and we explained to him that we were still operating as a family, that Joe and I discuss him and his sister every day.

We try to present a united front to the children, making the family's ground rules clear and consistent. This is particularly important in an unorthodox arrangement, since we break with convention in so many other ways. And since our arrangement doesn't look like most family setups, there are times when we have to stretch to find solutions to problems it presents, but we've found a balance that allows us to co-parent our children while retaining space to lead independent lives. When we get rattled, we remind ourselves what drew us to this solution in the first place, and we're okay. There are times when we find it necessary to reiterate the reasons: our children live with both of us full time, and we each have a better quality of life financially. If emotions or fatigue or frustration cloud our understanding of what we're doing, restating these simple facts helps us restore equilibrium.

༄

Dating is complicated in this new world of reconstructed families. Joe and I have both had new romantic partners. It hasn't been an issue for either of us, but we've learned to tread lightly where our children are concerned. It made our daughter uneasy when I began to date again. She worried that her dad would be lonely, and she looked askance at "the new guy." When a new woman entered her father's life, she relaxed. For the most part newcomers haven't been threatened by our arrangement, perhaps because they've seen their own share of sour separations. But what Joe and I are doing is not what is expected of separated couples, and that does present challenges and impose some limits on any new relationships we form. But what mid-life romance doesn't bring with it a set of complications of its own? Individuals rarely arrive solo. They, too, have families of their own, ex-partners they deal with, and baggage they carry around with them. A courtship at this stage of life must be a flexible one if it's going to work and be fair to everyone. Joe and I have always tried to make room for each other to live independent romantic lives and we've learned to acknowledge a broad spectrum of needs — ours, our children's, and those of our new partners and their families. Sometimes it's tricky to accommodate everyone's feelings and schedules, and sometimes we trip over our good intentions, but as long as we approach it with a sense of humor and a helpful attitude, we manage. Our children are our first priority until they're both fledged, and after that we'll renegotiate.

Life has begun to take on a somewhat predictable shape. Our family tree keeps growing — getting bigger, and producing more branches, and we try to spend big family events together — Christmas, Rosh Hashanah, Passover, Easter, and birthdays. One Christmas, my former mother-in-law, my sister, my children, my partner and his ex-wife and their daughter were all seated at my dining table. There have been many sweet moments; one year my long-distance beau was in town on Mother's Day, and he and I, Joe, the kids, and the dog all had brunch together. Joe and the kids have traditionally presented me with breakfast in bed on that day, so we modified the tradition and everyone gathered for a spring feast in the garden. I was aware of a slightly surreal quality to the situation, but everyone was happy to be there. Even after my long-distance romance faded, I continued a friendship with him and his ex-wife and daughter. The family tree becomes a little complicated to explain sometimes, and even I got tongue-tied when my ex-boyfriend's ex-wife's ex-girlfriend came to visit me and I was trying to introduce her to others.

It has now been more than four years since Joe and I separated, and we've eased into the new kind of complicated, unorthodox, flawed, and unfinished family we've become. I'm enormously proud of this work-in-progress that has given our kids one house, two proximal parents, and the knowledge that even the most serious disagreements can be managed. Initially, Joe and I made all this effort for our children, who had no choice but to come along for the ride. Lately though, I've begun to notice that something else is happening. The other morning, Joe and our daughter were sitting on my back steps while I bustled around the kitchen, and I overheard him tell her that he couldn't imagine life without Mommy in it. I silently thanked him for his generosity, not only for her sake, but for mine.

When we separated, Joe stopped giving me comic-strip gifts. But on my fiftieth birthday, a new one arrived. It documents our life as a reconstituted family, and while there is one image where we're squabbling a bit, there isn't a single frame in which I'm using my mouth as a weapon. As I looked at it, I realized that at last we've begun to find the friendship that eluded us in the tug-of-war that was our marriage.

I, too, wanted to celebrate our history together and our future as co-parents, so I took the eternity ring that Joe had given me on our tenth anniversary and had the diamonds reset in a new band that symbolized for me the evolving relation-ship with my ex-husband. I wear it with another circle of tiny diamonds that represents my enduring relationship with my children, and those two rings serve as a daily reminder of what matter mosts to me.

Conclusion

I DON'T WANT ANYONE TO THINK that the people you've met in this book are oddities. They're not. They're wonderfully ordinary people from a spectrum of backgrounds who, like growing numbers of people all over the world, are trying to create new families after a marriage dies. These are all people who've wrestled with pain, disappointment, and even betrayal, yet they've managed to deal with complex emotions, adapt to new circumstances, and preserve what was good about the relationships and the families they had built.

One family may bear little resemblance to another. Each may have its own limitations. Nonetheless, they all demonstrate what is possible with imagination, a generous spirit and an open heart, and all have managed to find a balance that worked for them. If there's one message this book affords, it's that even if romantic love doesn't last forever, the families we create do. And so do relationships with our partners — whatever the tone.

Divorcing couples often refer to their years together as "wasted," as time they threw away. Remarkably, most of the couples in this book have resisted that temptation, although it's easy to understand how it happens. We have been taught from the time we were tiny children that marriage is an endgame; once we get there, we are supposed to stay there. When marriage vows include the phrase "till death do us part," any other outcome signals failure.

The truth is that more than half of all marriages don't survive, but we still don't have positive models for dealing with this reality. We live with a kind of cognitive dissonance where we dream we will meet our prince charming or charming princess and live happily ever after, even when reality can't possibly measure up. And when it doesn't, we view separation and divorce as a disaster that demands rejection and severance instead of reorganization. What the stories in this book testify to is the fact that, while our lives may look different post-separation, they certainly don't have to be less than they once were.

Not long ago I came across the book *When Things Fall Apart* by Pema Chödrön, who became a Buddhist after her husband left her for another woman. "When that marriage fell apart," she wrote, "I tried hard — very, very hard — to go back to some kind of comfort, some kind of security, some kind of familiar resting place. Fortunately for me, I could never pull it off." Well, wouldn't we all like to crawl back into the comfort of what we imagined and hoped our lives would be? It's instinctive to want to avoid change, especially if it's uncomfortable and frightening, but our lives are always in transition and sometimes we're forced to adapt to circumstances we don't like. "Impermanence is the essence of everything," says Chödrön. "Impermanence is meeting and parting. It's falling in love and falling out of love. Impermanence is bittersweet, like buying a new shirt and years later finding it as part of a patchwork quilt."

We all live a patchwork kind of life, and all of our relationships go through various incarnations. When one incarnation, marriage, gives way to another, separation, we can choose how to respond. We can wallow in bitterness, or accept it as part of the continuum of a life. To do the latter, we'll have to let go of grudges, forgo petulance, and behave with the maturity grownups are supposed to possess, none of which is easy. However, it's worth the effort because the payoff is huge.

Inevitably, it is the children who pay the heaviest price when they are caught in the middle of their parents' battles. The adults in these stories made the simple but powerful commitment to put their children's needs ahead of their own and that played an integral part in the successful rebuilding of their families. Initially they did it for the the kids, but some of them, including me, were surprised to discover how much their own lives had been enriched by their domestic "experiments." Sometimes couples discovered that they were much better at being friends than marital partners, and where one relationship died, a new one bloomed and other kinds of love and friendship developed.

Everyone seeks some kind of family, connections with people they love, and each of us carries in our head an idealized notion of what a family — our family — should look like. We may grow up believing that a "family" is a mom and a dad and their kids all living under one roof, but that nuclear family is a Western concept that's less than a hundred years old. When we put the nuclear family on a pedestal as if it's *the* best structure within which to live, we set ourselves up for disappointment and frustration.

It's not the actual shape of the family that makes it work, it's the family's resilience, as Po Bronson observes in his book, *Why Do I Love These People?* "Sometimes this resilience shows itself in love that endures hurt. Occasionally the resilience takes the form of courage, as an individual breaks with tradition and starts a new family. At other times this resilience appears in the form of forgiveness." The same can be said of divorcing families: what matters most is that they find a shape that is flexible enough to be sustainable and strong enough to endure.

It's an idea that also comes up in Constance Ahrons's book, *The Good Divorce*. She says that separating couples wrestle with an overwhelming sense of private guilt and failure, but feel less like a failure and more like part of an emerging trend if they're able to see their situation in the larger context of evolving social mores. She talks about the emergence of a new family form, the bi-nuclear family, which she says "is rapidly becoming the most prevalent family form in our society." Marriages are going to end whether we like it or not and families have to rearrange themselves, so we might as well accept the reality and get on with it.

The families in this book looked to themselves for inspiration when it came to reconfiguring. By letting the shape of the new arrangements evolve from what felt right, they created families that best fit the needs and desires of their individual members. Megan's ex-husband Mike, who was fragile from two emotional breakdowns, was better off bunking in with his ex and extended family than going it alone in a grotty apartment, at a distance from his beloved daughter. He was able to draw on the support of his family when his teenage son, JT, needed to straighten out his own life. Alone he might not have had the resources. Alan and Maria's collaboration in an upstairs/downstairs arrangement enabled them to surmount their testy relationship and cobble together a peaceful environment in which their daughters can live with both of them.

Marjorie Harris, who pioneered separate households many years ago with her ex-husband, Jack Batten, agrees that we shouldn't try to squeeze ourselves into a model of life that may not fit our own particular needs or wants. "When you start off with a rule or an image of this ideal of perfection, it gets battered too easily. You know, you've *got to* behave this way, you've *got to* have this ritual . . . it's 'got to' rather than 'why?' and 'where are we going?'" Harris escaped a traditional family she found stifling by creating a unique arrangement that worked for her and her ex-husband. "I wasn't so much anti-marriage, I just was anti the *convention* of marriage. I didn't really care what anybody thought. I was absorbed with the idea of 'Isn't this an exciting thing to do? Isn't it an interesting way to see another unfolding of your life and your relationships?' I was doing something for me, and it was good for him, too."

Like Harris, the people in this book have questioned convention, eschewing commonly accepted ways of dealing with their problems and believing instead that they'd know what they needed for their families. The process of remaking a family is intense and confusing, and couples need to be forgiving of their imperfections and weaknesses while continuing to move toward solutions.

Since most of us are novices when we take the first steps toward severing marital arrangements, we tend to seek help from the "experts" we hope will guide us, but no one knows our children better than we do. Instead of racing out to find an expert to resolve internal issues, we can sit down together at the kitchen table and establish our own priorities, sorting things according to what we both believe to be important.

In my own case, my ex and I have been able to establish post-separation financial arrangements that are based entirely on trust. Eventually we will do a "kitchen-table" divorce where we work out the details on our own and then have it checked to make sure it's legally binding. While not everyone can do that, for us it has worked extremely well. Other couples, especially those who have complicated financial lives, may need the security of an agreement that from the start is spelled out on paper. Some might benefit from assistance in working out new financial and legal arrangements, and there are planners and lawyers who can do that without escalating negotiations into a turf battle. Financial issues are always delicate and fraught with past history, so it is important to embrace a way to resolve them that makes both partners feel safe and secure. Whatever is agreed upon should be checked by a lawyer to ensure that it's legal and enforceable. Remember, though, that in the end, an agreement on paper is only as useful as the willingness between two people to honor it.

༄

My own observation and experience have convinced me that we should take as our mantra, "marriages end, families don't." We should repeat it again and again to ourselves, and say it to our families and friends when they express doubts about what we're doing. After four years of successfully sharing a house with my ex-husband, I still encounter people who look at me as though I'm joking when I explain my living arrangement. Over time I've realized that those who express disbelief or skepticism are often projecting their own bitter experiences onto what we're doing. Their judgments rattled me in the early days of our separation and I found myself becoming unsure of our wisdom. Now that I've lived it and heard about others' experiences, I feel confident that the approach we've taken is correct for us. Of course it's one thing to repeat a mantra and quite another to live by it. It takes patience, long-term vision, and a wagonload of good-heartedness to build a new family with someone we no longer wish to be married to. When emotions are high and animosities smoulder and everyone is assailed by conflicting loyalties, old grievances can surface in surprising ways.

ᴄ⳽ꝿ

Divorcing amicably and building a new family structure requires more than just making peace with each other. It also means ignoring the pessimists around you. The other day I ran into an old friend who's been crafting a new relationship with his partner, and he was regaling me with stories about how outsiders have reacted to their decision to stay in the same house. He's moved to the basement, they share the kitchen, and they're still sorting out what to do long term but, in the short run, the arrangement allows them both to remain fully involved in co-parenting their daughter. He's encountered doubting Thomases who, never having done it themselves, weigh in on the weakness of his arrangement, citing possible calamity as a result of money issues, new love interests arriving on the scene, or one partner exploiting or taking advantage of the other. While all of these are *possible* sources of conflict, they are not *necessary* ones, especially when there is a level of trust. And thankfully, the skeptics aren't in the majority. Whenever I tell my story to a group of people, someone will invariably volunteer information about another "unusual" family. There are lots of us out there, I've discovered, but our stories haven't been documented before.

Friends and family can feel awkward and protective when relationships break down. Meaning to be supportive they take sides, not realizing that cheerleading for the person they see as aggrieved is more likely to hinder than help. Marriage breakdown is often viewed as a crime with a victim and a perpetrator, but the truth of any marriage is more complex than that, and divorce should not be about winning a battle. Even if you see your ex-partner as the villain, your children most likely do not. If there's ongoing conflict, everyone loses — especially the children — and it befits the adults to behave as maturely as possible and to manage the anger, seek counseling, and move on.

I've seen from my own experience, and from that of the children I've interviewed, that youngsters aren't automatically damaged if their parents' relationship didn't work out, but they surely suffer if their parents engage in cheap shots or wage all-out war with each other. Constance Ahrons has recently published a book titled *We're Still Family: What Grown Children Have to Say About Their Parents' Divorce.* In it she describes a study she did twenty years earlier chronicling the divorce experiences of ninety-eight families. She subsequently interviewed 173 of the now-adult children and found that in most cases the parents' divorce wasn't a defining factor in how the kids turned out. Conflict, more than separation, is what throws kids off balance. "Loyalty conflicts always produce distress," Ahrons says. "Children hate to put one parent above the other. If they side with one parent, it means they must now side against the other. They are keenly aware that when they've hurt one parent, or pushed one parent away, they are shutting out one parent's love." The old expression "shame the parent, shame the child" holds true, and what matters above all is "establishing a cooperative partnership that permits the bonds of kinship to continue."

Children whose families metamorphose into new shapes become quite sophisticated about what a family can include. Ahrons found in her interviews that most children of divorce had learned to manage changes to their families as their parents dated, cohabited, remarried, and sometimes re-divorced. Psychologically, the children were developmentally on target. "Although they went through difficult times, and experienced stressful family changes, most emerged stronger and wiser in spite of — or perhaps because of — their complex histories." In other words, if parents managed well, the children could too.

In my generation, having divorced parents was outside the norm and carried a kind of stigma. These days, divorced families are commonplace. I once did a tally of eight of my daughter's friends, and only one had parents who were still together as a couple. To those kids, that's just how it was, no big deal. What might not have been quite so typical is that most of their parents had established fairly genial relations with each other.

Establishing a new family model can be a delicate balancing act, easily threatened by conflict. Our daughter would rush to interrupt anything she feared was a potentially dangerous dispute. She would become furious with us for allowing any friction to surface, and I eventually realized she was afraid that if we had a disagreement, our entire new family arrangement would tumble like a house of cards. It has taken time for her to believe that if her father and I disagree on something, we will work it out. We've learned to be very careful about how we discuss thorny issues because while *we* know that we'll find our way to a compromise, *she* hasn't always been confident of that. So we step lightly in this area and she's become notice-ably more relaxed about it, too. When we do things together as a family, she and her brother love it. We often have family dinners together, sharing stories and laughing, and to this day the most delicious moments between us are when we all collapse in a heap over someone's goofy joke or folly.

Every family has its own set of traditions and rituals, and these should be treasured, even after a couple splits up. They "help define our lives, make sense of our history, partially determine our future, and help us connect with one another," according to Ahrons. Where one tradition is lost or changes, a new one should be created to take its place. The many members of the family with the kitty corner houses upheld a tradition of family meetings that allowed them to hammer out their differences. They also chose to gather most nights for dinner together and everyone was expected to lay down their tools for that time. Darlene and Tom established a family ritual of taking turns hosting a weekly movie and games night with their daughter, and that evening together was sacrosanct for them. Marc continues to make coffee every morning for his ex-wife Mary, a ritual she adores, and together they created a new tradition on the first anniversary following their breakup by moving their wedding rings to their right hands and recommitting themselves to each other.

Maintaining rituals can be delicate business, however. The wider social expectation is that when a marriage ends, the ex is cut out of the other family's activities. You'll have your Christmas turkey and he'll have his Passover Seder. It doesn't have to be that way. In our case, it took a little while for all of us to adjust to how to handle extended family events. As it turned out, the children adapted more quickly than the grownups. Our kids still see us as an intact family, and they laid down the law that if one of their parents wasn't invited to the other's parties, the kids wouldn't go. Now we are both included in family festivities. There have, it is true, been delicate moments when we have had to be sensitive to the feelings of new partners coming into our clan, and some issues have been quite challenging. Becoming part of an unusual family can be unnerving for the new person, as Sue found out when she had to stake out her own place within the sprawling group of "Type-A" characters in the "kitty-corner" family.

What we build with our ex makes sense to *us* because it's partly informed by how we lived as a family before the separation. New people who come into the picture bring their own experiences with them and sometimes a little baggage from their own past. Everyone has to adjust, give a little, and cede some territory, and insecurities can manifest themselves in ways that are sometimes difficult to understand but which need to be acknowledged.

The unorthodox arrangements in this book required greater overlap between old and new worlds, although the benefits of becoming part of a bigger family were not always readily apparent to everyone. In several of the families, the children admitted to initially resenting their parents' new partners, but now say how much they appreciate having them in their lives.

Keeping the divorce process in the hands of the couple who are splitting up has a great deal of merit. I once interviewed a lawyer who for twenty years had successfully specialized in family law. After winning a very challenging divorce case one day, her elation evaporated the instant she saw her client's face. As she turned to congratulate him, he responded, "If we won, why do I feel like I lost?" His son no longer spoke to him and his relationship with his ex-wife was in tatters. That lawyer now specializes in collaborative practice, a new branch of law in which lawyers and clients agree not to take the case to court, and all decisions are made in joint meetings between the couple and their legal representatives. There are no backroom meetings or ultimatums. In addition to the lawyers, the process includes family therapists, financial planners and mediators, and while it's not an inexpensive option, it's much cheaper, and more civilized, than litigation.

Managing conflicting emotions, particularly in the midst of anger, hurt and frustration, is difficult, but it can be done and done well. I remember a friend who was going through a divorce wryly quoting from Nietzsche: "What does not kill you makes you stronger." That same friend told me that every day he'd remind himself of what he hoped his family would look like after he and his wife had separated — that they'd all stay connected and have dinner together every Sunday. It was his vision of a future, and holding on to it helped him avoid getting distracted by things that, in the end, were unimportant. One of my friends advised me to "breathe" through some of the really stressful moments and though it sometimes required a Herculean effort, I realize looking back that my ex was doing the same thing — biting his tongue, quietly trying to regain his composure, avoiding the old conflict-ridden situations. Some of the other families in these chapters had to make the opposite effort, learning how to express their feelings instead of withdrawing into silence. What all of us learned is that friction, intensity, anger, and pain can be managed and will pass with time.

Time is your friend, and it's very important to learn to trust it. I'm impatient by nature but my sister, thinking of the way time flows, would counsel me "not to push the river." It took awhile before I understood that each difficult moment is only that — a moment in time. Our wise therapist suggested another way of trusting time, by putting conflict into an imaginary composter, then returning to it more calmly when the conflict had subsided. We can't avoid the pain, but we can control how we deal with it.

Anne Lamott wrote a memoir called *Bird by Bird* in which she tells a story about her ten-year-old brother who had been assigned a school project on birds. He procrastinated so long that he became overwhelmed as the due date loomed. He was in tears until, as Lamott describes it, "my father sat down beside him, put his arm around my brother's shoulder, and said, 'Bird by bird, buddy. Just take it bird by bird.'" As the people in these pages made their way through the uncharted, sometimes rough, terrain of their new lives, each in their own way employed that simple wisdom. I still have the phrase "bird by bird" on a sticky note that's attached to my computer monitor where I can see it every day.

When we have to reconfigure the family structure, we should take it step by step, trusting our own instincts and trying to remember that we're forever linked to the father or mother of our offspring. We are the only two people in the world with that relationship, and there's something to be cherished in that. The people in this book have reshaped their families in ways that respect and honor each member of the clan, and each has placed the children first in the hierarchy of needs and importance in the family, recognizing that there's no one correct model for living, no one shape that a family should take. The arrangements these families have made can be fragile, and they might not work for you or me, but that's okay. They work for *them*, and that's what counts. Perhaps the most important lesson I've learned through my own experience, and one from which we all can benefit, is this: don't mourn what you've lost; invest your energies in building with what you have and you may surprise yourself with what is possible.

Families

These are the families who have shared their stories for this book. In some cases, 'going public' with the details of their lives is sensitive, and in one chapter I've used pseudonyms to protect their privacy. In another, only first names appear. I have noted where this happens. Otherwise, real names are used throughout this book.

CHAPTER FOUR
All in the Family

Megan Brown, Mike Brown

Children
Amie Brownbridge, Bethan Brown, JT Brown

New Partner
Bill Brown

Mike's first wife
Margaret McCabe

CHAPTER FIVE
Forgive us our Trespasses
NOTE: Starred names are pseudonyms.

Allison Loucks, Andrew*

New Partners
Elizabeth*, Kurt Loucks

Children
AJ*

CHAPTER SIX
Domestic Détente

Maria Fazari, Allan Johnson

Children
Amelia Johnson, Michela Johnson, Olivia Johnson

CHAPTER SEVEN
No More Secrets
NOTE: This family requested that their surname not be used.

Mark, Mary

Children
Kate, Madeleine

CHAPTER EIGHT
Crossing the Rubicon

Peter McGee, LJ Nelles

Children
Sarah Nelles-McGee, Taylor Nelles-McGee
New Partner
Jon Gal

CHAPTER NINE
A House Divided

Tom Coyle, Anna MacKay-Smith

Children
Matthew Coyle, Nicholas Coyle, Samantha (Sam) Coyle

CHAPTER TEN
Reconcilable Differences

Cate Cochran, Joseph (Joe) Sherman

Children
Madeline (Maddie) Cochran, Jacob (Jake) Sherman

Acknowledgments

I AM DEEPLY INDEBTED to the families in this book, who shared their stories with candor and courage, demonstrating that there is always more than one way to solve a problem. I am grateful for their generosity and impressed that they opened the doors and windows on their personal lives.

Margie Wolfe, my publisher, was the first to suggest that I do a book on the subject and I have her to thank for the birth of this work. Her vibrant enthusiasm and some wonderful breakfasts kept me going on the harder days of writing. Carolyn Jackson's deft and gentle hand made the editing process painless and Melissa Kaita was a delight to work with on the design. The women of Second Story Press were always accommodating and welcoming and I thank them all.

A version of Chapter Ten first appeared in *Toronto Life* magazine, where it was edited by Sarah Fulford. I am very appreciative of her editorial rigor and guidance.

My ex-husband, Joseph Sherman, was a real mensch to allow me to expose his personal life to public scrutiny. He is a very private person and I thank him for his goodhearted-ness and his wonderful illustrations. He and I are becoming old hands at this new life and are better friends now than we were when we were married. Not a day passes when I don't feel thankful that he and I are raising kids together.

Our children, Maddie and Jake, are the reason we're doing this, and throughout they have been little beacons of hope. Maddie, who is wise beyond her years, helps keep us on track with her fierce commitment to this family. If we falter, she chides us and we listen. Jake, who came into life testing limits and saying no! has emerged as a gracious young man of many yeses. His enduring faith in our family, whatever its shape, has kept us on track and his good humor has lightened our efforts.

My parents are the inspiration for most of the things I do in my life. My father, Sandy, taught me the importance of honesty and dignity, and my mother, Janet, has been my role model for just about everything. Her indefatigable enthusiasm, intelligence, and perseverance have taught me to question conventional wisdom and, in the truest sense, she and I are kindred spirits. But of equal importance, in terms of this book my mother is a great editor. She and I worked on this book as a team, and her eyes were the first and last to see every single word I've written. Her contribution is immeasurable, as is my gratitude, and this is really *our* book, not just mine.

My beloved sister, Anne, is a sustaining force in my life,

and I thank her for giving me her "writing cabin" and for helping me see that there's life after every disaster.

My ex-in-laws, Nicki, Minda, Steve and their children, and my "favorite mother-in-law," Harriet, have never wavered in embracing Joe's and my new relationship and for this I salute them.

To my friends, old and new, I owe a huge debt, including Ines Buchli and Talin Vartanian, both of whom introduced me to families in this book, Schuster Gindin, Barbara Kerr, Karen Levine, Jane Mingay, Peter Thillaye and Ellen Vanstone, among so many others. I have no idea what I would do without them. I owe a special thank you to Ralph Cameron Martin.

For the ways that they helped facilitate the writing process, I thank the Ontario Arts Council for two writing grants; Penny Freedom for the use of her "ice house" by the ocean; Dorothy Harvey and Ron Dahmer for helping me work at MacGregor Bay; Robert Kerr for the use of "The Landing;" Elizabeth Shein for the loan of her yellow "beetle;" Robert Wilmot for the chair and wildflowers; John Lute for the music and the loan of Aberdeen Farm; Wendy Dennis for her early editorial input; Nehal El-Hadi, Ian Godfrey, and Rebecca Valero for patiently transcribing dozens of hours of taped interviews; my colleagues at CBC Radio's *The Sunday Edition* for their cheerful support, particularly Lynda Shorten for being a wonderfully flexible boss; and Sheila Willson for her ongoing guidance, without which my life would not be the same.